The
Demon of Progress
in the Arts

The
Demon of Progress
in the Arts

by

WYNDHAM LEWIS

Henry Regnery Company

Chicago, Illinois, 1955

CONTENTS

v

PLATES

Between pages 50 and 51

Bombelli

Engel-Pak

Between pages 58 and 59

Michael Ayrton

Francis Bacon

Robert Colquhoun

John Minton

INTRODUCTION

Introduction

I

EXTREMISM is not easy to define or to describe. It is a disease like foot and mouth disease, which disastrously visits, not cattle, but artists. It is a disease which appeared, for the first time, among European artists, not more than fifty years ago. The kinds of artist among which the symptoms were most easily identified were the painter and the sculptor. It is not, however, a virus to which the visual artist, and no other, is susceptible. It was an accident that it was among them that it first manifested itself. The first case to be reported in these islands was mine, around 1913. You may imagine the sensation created—it was like the first Colorado beetle to be spotted in our rich brown fields, clinically free of odious sub-tropical pests.

Fortunately, with me the disease did not have time to mature. Another scourge, namely war, intervened. While, in one way and another, suffering from this martial pestilence I began to think a little. I recognized that, prior to the war, I had been visited by a complaint of a most unusual kind. I saw that it was irrational to attempt to transmute the art of painting into music—to substitute for the most naturally concrete of the arts the most inevitably abstract. So of course I recovered my reason. This did not mean that I abandoned a twentieth-century way of seeing. I escaped—that was all— from reaching a point, very soon, where I should have ceased to be a *visual* artist at all. For what I was headed for, obviously, was to fly away from the world of men, of pigs, of chickens and alligators, and to go to live in the unwatered moon, only a moon sawed up into square blocks, in the most alarming way. What an escape I had!

But to take up the question of this disease again: its identification is not always by any means easy, which is one of the

3

most dangerous things about it. It is difficult not to mistake it for something else. It has nothing whatever to do with art, but it resembles so closely one of the most common conditions experienced by artists.

There are, indeed, several intellectual excesses in no way pathologic—strainings towards the untried, which must have existed in paleolithic times as much as in our own. For *extremism*, this deadly disease about which I am writing, very closely resembles, at first sight, and to the untutored eye, that healthy originality by which an artist is properly exhilarated when he notices it—that sort of deep and honourable *difference* which marks out a Franz Hals, a Magnasco, a Goya, among all his fellows—which is a hallmark as real as a birthmark; and which is the *only* advantage over others which is worth having.

I hope you will believe me when I say that I am quite sure that the English school making its appearance during World War Two, and just after, is actually the finest group of painters and sculptors which England has ever known. I do not refer to achievement; I refer to the existence of so many people who understand painting, and who have revealed a high order of attainment. The Pre-Raphaelites (the only other comparable collection of artists) were parochial by comparison; this group is European.

Let me name a few: Ayrton, Bacon, Colquhoun, Craxton, Minton, Moore, Passmore, Richards, Sutherland, Trevelyan.[1] Except Henry Moore the sculptor, and Graham Sutherland (though older, an integral part of this school), all of these are still young enough for me to be able to say perhaps the maximum effort has not been put forth: so let me only speak of the *quality* of which there has been unmistakable evidence in all of these painters. A combination of the *Musée Sans Murs* and of the Golden Arrow, which so quickly wafts one to Paris, has made all these artists as good as Paris-trained. This may

[1] There are others, but I select those with whose work I am very familiar because of my 'Round the Galleries' articles in *The Listener*.

account for a quality which is as mature and well-equipped as if this were a band of Bretons rather than merely Britons. In looking back upon my weekly tour of the shows at the time of my *Listener* articles, hundreds of canvases are crowded together in my memory, from each of which I received authentic delight, which only a work of the first order is capable of producing. I remember with what enchantment I came upon a group of paintings by Trevelyan at the Galleries of Gimpel Fils, for I was not very familiar with his work; Ceri Richards' pianoforte pieces; Craxton's tank for bathing at the foot of a steep hotel; Ayrton's superb portrait of William Walton composing, the striations of the figure rhythmically associated with the vertically striated cliff—a portrait which should find its place in the National Portrait Gallery; a Colquhoun portrait, of a splendid density, in the hall of the late D. Macdonald's flat, which is still vividly present to me; the water-colour vegetation of the grandest quality, a small thing by Minton; Passmore (now in great danger), a snow-lighted Thames expanse, a glittering vibration, an invention of the first order; the bitter verdure of the gallows-tree, in preparation for a Crucifixion, by Sutherland.

Now, for the average gallery-goer, each and all of these painters is an extremist—an authentic extremist. In a sense, of course, they are; but not in any way the kind of extremist I am talking about in this book. None of them is touched, even, by that contagion that hurries an artist to zero and to the death of talent. And here is where the gallery-gazer has to sharpen his wits and see the gulf that lies between painters of this sort, and those who are passing over into the rocky path upon the edge of the abyss—that ultimate advance-of-all-advances, where there is no more advance because there is *nothing*.

When I consider this gifted mass, not one but a dozen superb image-makers, capable of almost anything, I shudder at the thought of that withering disease which might at any

moment attack them (the pictures of one are already turning
to wood, but he is a man of heroic mould, and I believe that
he will, one day, set fire to his carpentry). But an apocalypse
takes shape in my anxious mind. I see with horror Francis
Bacon's elephants being stricken with extremism, grown ashen
and transparent, their trunks drooping, and falling in a heap
of white ashes at the foot of their canvas, livid and vast and
blank. That is not all. Mildly monumental, grandly sculpted,
I perceive, aghast, some work of Moore's, as beautifully defined as a thundercloud, suddenly dissolving into an absurd
abstraction, until at last there is nothing left of it but a
phantom sausage, convulsed and withering into a white head-
less worm, a beginning of nothing. Everywhere the beginnings
of nothing. I see the noble form of a Pompeii of Minton's silted
up with the volcanic void, the concrete nothingness that comes
from the fires beneath the crust. How terrifyingly destructive!
—I could behold with more equanimity an apocalypse of hops,
a blank desuetude ensuing from the consumption of that
British national drink closely resembling urine. I could be an
unmoved witness perhaps, of this generation, blossoming in
many images, dissolving in a dull orgy of British beer. Perhaps
I could stolidly observe this brood of brilliant painters stricken
with a black vomiting which I recognized as the plague. I have
experienced so much that is exceptionally tragic that, were
they all gathered in the Festival Hall, by some mischance, to
listen to a new symphony by Mr. Britten, and should the hall
be struck, and set on fire by a meteorite, and should they all
perish in the flames, I should be horrified, but I should see
that God did not mean England to have painters, and I would
accept this, perhaps, as another example of those actions of
the divinity which we find it impossible to comprehend.

But there is something which would affect me quite differently. I should be terribly moved if I had to be present at the
spectacle of the graven and painted riches of the work of their
hands blotted out; all their subtly imagined forms engulfed in
a pretentious intellectualist abstraction. There is something

peculiarly diabolic about all the concentration of selective
energy, all the beauty of the mind embalmed in some great
carving, deformed in the name of art, 'abstracted' into nothing
to satisfy some collective vanity.

II

A last preliminary elucidation concerning this mad bug
which has entered into the body of the arts. The first and the
last thing to say to make my meaning clear is that the extremism in question has nothing whatever to do with progress
—with advance. In this essay I have made use of the word
extremism because that is how it would be described by most
people. It may help a little if I provide the reader with a
parallel taken from another department of life, one of purely
mechanical creation. Suppose the best-known firm of aeroplane
manufacturers began advertising the first model of a wonder-
plane, one which would far excel any it had so far produced.
After months of boosting and plugging, at last this hush-hush
wonder-plane comes on the market. Everywhere it comes to the
test: test pilots everywhere are testing it out—and all die—
within five minutes of taking off. And naturally the most
infernal uproar ensues.

This wonder-plane is now subjected to an examination of
the most elaborate kind, and it is not long before a report is
issued, sensational in the extreme. It has been established that,
in the heart of the mechanism, there is a fault, almost impossible to detect, which absolutely guarantees that the plane
will rise easily into the air, and then, once it is there, will, in
the same moment, turn over and plunge earthwards, into a
crash in which both machine and man are utterly consumed.

The ingenuity of this death-trap amazes all the experts. The
newspapers, we can easily imagine, print no other news until
the explanation of this ghastly event is forthcoming.

Only one solution can be found; that alone is sufficiently
awful to correspond with the awful facts. Not only the designer

of the plane, but the managing-director of the aeroplane works, and every expert in this great establishment, is obviously criminally insane.

Imagine what the newspapers look like at this point! All the psychiatrists in the country are asked to provide an explanation of how this MASS LUNACY (as, in banner headlines, the press describes it) could have occurred. The most brilliant and resourceful of the massed mad-doctors, while admitting that no case of collective homicidal lunacy of quite this order has ever been recorded, comes forward with a theory. He would say, 'What, to start with, does this fearful crime oblige me to agree as the only possible motive?' The learned doctor can see nothing for it but that *an intense, an insane hatred of flying* was at the bottom of this diabolical action, involving the certainty of at least a dozen men being gripped by this phobia, and revealing to one another how they loathed their occupation; how they detested the air, and everything to do with it. That they conspired together to abolish flying, once and for all, is quite evident. Finally, there is universal speculation as to whether flying will be responsible, in future, for other examples of this contagious mania. Should I add that the twelve convicted engineers and contractors will be confined, *en masse*, in Broadmoor.

Now painting, alas, may be productive of manias just as rabid as one can imagine flight might lead to (or, if you wish for a more obvious possible incentive for dementia, the manufacture of the atomic bomb). The question of human life is not involved. Even if it could be proved that many people were possessed of a consuming hatred of art in general, and of oil-paintings and of sculpture of figures in stone and wood in particular, no conviction would ensue. There is nothing in criminal law, I believe, to send a man to the gallows for plotting the wholesale destruction of works of art; or, more compendiously, planning the abolition of all culture, and all man's historic arts.

If, in the windows of the art dealers, all that were to be seen

were a few white empty canvases (and it may not be long before
that is precisely what we shall see), and if, in answer to the
enquiries of the newspapers' representatives, the dealer were
curtly to reply that "this is the latest kind of 'movement'",
all this should evoke no surprise. I am explaining to you in
these pages what is occurring, and why.

III

Finally, let me give you an illustration of how painting is
productive of aberration, even in a powerful mind. Let me
quote a little from a well-known passage in Ruskin's *Stones of
Venice*, in which, in the most violent manner, he is denouncing
all the painting from and including the Italian Renaissance.

Instant degradation followed in every direction—a flood of folly
and hypocrisy. Mythologies, ill-understood at first, then perverted
into feeble sensualities, take the place of the representation of Christian subjects, which had become blasphemous under the treatment
of men like the Caracci. Gods without power, satyrs without rus-
ticity, nymphs without innocence, men without humanity, gather
into idiot groups upon the polluted canvas, and scenic affectations
encumber the streets with preposterous marble. Lower and lower
declines the level of abused intellect; the base school of landscape
gradually usurps the place of the historical painting, which had sunk
into prurient pedantry,—the Alsatian sublimities of Salvator, the
confectionery idealities of Claude, the dull manufacture of Gaspar
and Canaletto, south of the Alps, and in the north the patient devo-
tion of besotted lives to delineation of bricks and fogs, cattle and
ditchwater.[1]

This unrestrained onslaught of Ruskin's, ending in the
magnificent 'cattle and ditchwater', is an excellent example
of the extent to which painting may produce in a man a bitter
hatred of entire schools, and the art of a number of countries.
Now, believe it or not, *all* representation—all pictures, not
only of cattle and ditches, but of every visual scene or image,

---

[1] *Stones of Venice*, Vol. I, p. 38.

end by enraging some men, until they denounce every picture and every statue in the world. It is not only Plato who is moved to hatred by *imitation* in the arts. On the contrary, such an objection to all imitation of nature, to all those arts which conjure up a scene, or make a person stand before you, either in paint or stone, is lunatic, I think, but as common as homicide.

Is this extremism about which I have been speaking the result of an aberration such as I have described above? Is it a case in which only zero is tolerated—in which nothing is preferred to something? It would, I am afraid, be flattering all the pundits and painters engaged in those enterprises if we explained what they did in that way. It is where there is *no* excuse of this kind, but only vanity and silliness, that one is moved to curse these impostors for the death of art which they are attempting to achieve.

Part I

HOW THE ARTS DIFFER IN THEIR EXTREMISM

I

Music less Extreme than Fine Arts

MUSIC in England is not so dominated by the *snobisme* of what is 'advanced' as are the visual arts. There is no 'advanced' musician, dodecaphonic or otherwise, who has attained to anything like the pre-eminence among musicians that Picasso occupies among artists. The visual arts are a form of expression more remote from the popular than is music or indeed any other art; and so the visual arts have been able to proceed with 'advances' of an extreme and spectacular kind in a way that music could not, even if it wanted to.

At the present moment the most generally acceptable musician in England, is, I suppose, Benjamin Britten. Benjamin Britten compares himself with Purcell and with Mozart; although these two great masters of music would no doubt be vastly surprised, in listening to *Billy Budd*, to learn that its author considered himself closely akin to them, nevertheless there is the will to be *classic*. He is not a man claiming to have far surpassed and outdistanced the great classics, and to have attained to distant regions of expression in a different dimension altogether from that of the old masters, as do contemporary artists. No, no one (either other musicians or the public) expects that of him. They are satisfied that he should be as good as Purcell or as Mozart. Whereas painters and sculptors are whisked away into an arcanum by a host of pundits, a wild competition of 'advancedness' takes them entirely out of sight of the public. Their position is a far less natural, and, I believe, a less healthy one than is that of the musician.

If it were on the basis of competitive and snobbish 'advancedness' that we were to look for the most contemporary musician in England, I suppose we would take Mátyás Seiber.

But he is largely unknown to any but musicians. If contemporary, in matters of music, signified the kind of 'advancedness' which is accepted as a criterion of value in the visual arts, then one would have to place William Walton higher than Benjamin Britten, simply because Walton's compositions had been nearer than are Britten's to the dodecaphonic school of Germany. Upon a line of advance of that kind, if it were accepted as an ascent, Hindemith (Walton's particular inspiration), although miles behind Alban Berg, is higher up than Purcell or Mozart (those poor old classicists at the bottom of the scale)—and therefore more acceptable as a 'contemporary'. Upon this vertical scale of valuation Benjamin Britten could reach no higher —be no more contemporary—than a follower of Richard Wagner, say Erich Korngold.

Let me say that, when I say popular, I mean *snobbishly accepted*; for, in all the arts, what we term popular signifies a selective audience, removed from and very much smaller than the general public.

Confining ourselves to the English cultural scene, we have an extremely vivid illustration of the phenomenon I have been discussing in the small-time promoter and pundit, Mr. Edward Clark, and what was, until recently, the London Contemporary Music Centre, of which he was chairman. Clark, who for five years studied in Germany under Schoenberg, was probably the main and sole adherent of extremism in music in this country. If he could have his way composers of the type of Alban Berg would have the same standing as such artists as Henry Moore have in the visual field. As long ago as the 'twenties, Mr. Edward Clark organized a series of chamber concerts in the Aeolian Hall at which Schoenberg's *Pierrot Lunaire* and Stravinsky's *Histoire du Soldat* were performed. He is the most consistent and persistent would-be mobilizer of musical extremism in England. Had the musical world in England been as much in agreement with him as the art-world had been in agreement with Sir Herbert Read, Mr. Edward Clark would have been Sir Edward Clark, he would have had at his disposal considerable

sums of money, he would have been the president of an institute, predominantly musical. As it is, what do we see? The
London Contemporary Music Centre and its chairman have
disappeared, or rather have been swallowed bodily by the
Institute of Contemporary Arts, the president of which is Sir
Herbert Read (knighted last year). This is a glaring confirm-
ation of what I have been expounding above, regarding the
respective positions of musical extremism and of extremism in
the fine arts in Great Britain.

To summarize: to be musically 'contemporary' in England
is to be something like Benjamin Britten; unless you wish to
ignore entirely the majority trend. And what the pre-eminence
in music of Benjamin Britten—backward-looking, classicist in
intention—signifies, can perhaps be best seen by considering
what the visual arts would look like, who would be the domin-
ant figure, if the conditions there were the same as in music.
In that case Augustus John (backward-looking and in intention
classicist or at least traditional), or some artist of that kind,
and with as much power, would be cock of the walk, as John
was forty years ago. It would be an incredibly different scene
from that presented by the London art world today, which has
just caught up with continental extremism.

II

A Brake on Musical Extremism

THE great disparity between music and the fine arts, in the matter of advancedness, is a circumstance which, personally, I have not seen discussed, though I am sure it must be something that musical extremists like Mr. Edward Clark are well aware of, and must be very sore about. As to an analysis of the reasons for this disparity, I know of none, and yet it is of very great interest to anyone investigating the history of extremism in the various arts.

To undertake a complete analysis of this would be a big job. In the first place, any expressive sound, like music, has a great deal of psychological affinity with the human voice. The painted image, sculpted wood or stone is quite a different matter; it has no direct emotional appeal. Everything that follows and is connected with this central fact would have to be examined first.

Economics provides a very substantial asset towards the solution of this problem. It may weigh more heavily against extremism than anything else, that there is a vast army of instrumentalists, which we may call the rank-and-file army of instrumental music. The interests of this horde of instrumentalists are protected by a powerful trade union. These instrumentalists are essential to many theatres, to great numbers of hotels, to dance halls, to performances of all sorts, to opera, to ballet, broadcasting, etc. Now the rank and file of all these orchestras, large and small, favour what is normal and popular in music. Their bread and butter depends upon music which is normal and popular. Their livelihood would be menaced if most musical composers indulged in types of composition calculated to drive away the public.

16

Imagine the habitués of the Proms being assailed during every concert by dodecaphonic numbers. Or think of lunchers and diners having to listen to the compositions of Schoenberg or of Berg or something even more cacophanous, more wounding to the ear. They would protest to the management that if such displeasing sounds continued to be made by the hotel orchestra, they would go for their meals somewhere else. This would be the reaction in every case where dodecaphonic austerities were substituted for music: very soon all the orchestral players would be on the streets, earning their living by regaling the passers-by with delightful tunes.

Here we have, I feel quite sure, one compelling reason for the normality—the lack of extremism—in contemporary music. Musical composers are restrained from giving rein, for whatever reason, to their harsher impulses. That enormous army of hungry instrumentalists is a very big factor in holding music back from 'advances' of the type of Reg Butler.

How much more expensive an art is music than painting or sculpture is proved by the budget of the Arts Council, the details of which are set down in its annual report. In the departments into which the Arts Council is divided, the annual expenditure of the department of music far exceeds that of all other departments. The subsidy set aside for financing the ballet and the opera is four or five times as much as the quite modest sum required for the upkeep of the visual arts department.

III

What it Costs to have Music

THERE is no parallel at all between what it costs the State
to fill the gap caused by the vanishing of private patronage
in the case of the fine arts, and in that of music. The reason for
the colossal expenditure involved in putting on a ballet, or
making an opera possible, is easy to understand, when you
consider the cost of the rent of the theatre, the weekly salaries
of a large orchestra, the even greater expenditure in the
combined salaries of a massive cast of performers, with the
necessary quota of stars, not to mention the choreographers,
producers, etc., the costumes, the scenery, the heating and
lighting, box office and theatre staff, advertising, etc. etc. No
such expense as this is involved in keeping a painter at his
easel, or providing a sculptor with a piece of wood, a lump of
clay, or a block of stone. There are not many of these artists
worth supporting, painters or sculptors. No state in its senses
would wish to support more than a couple of dozen of them.
The only material they use, that has any value at all, is marble.
There is no art so independent of money as the visual arts.

If we turn to another art, that of the cinema, we have at
once a kind of creation which is fabulously expensive, right
from the start. I refer, of course, to what is, for the cinematograph, the same as paper or canvas for the painter—namely
celluloid. There is no more expensive basic material for an
expressive art in the world. I once listened to Mr. Grierson,
king of documentaries, expounding the economic problems
confronting any man who used the cinematograph camera. I
was amazed and horrified to learn what it cost to produce even
a short documentary film.

In contrast to this a great masterpiece of one of the visual

18

arts, an exquisite water-colour by J. W. Turner, or of Edward Lear (better known as the nonsense rhymer), costs nothing to make—a few shillings. Such facts as these are of the greatest significance in understanding the line of development of the fine arts in our day, in contrast with the other arts. The fact that a painter can embark upon an easel-picture of considerable size with an expense of only a few pounds—that the creation of a major work of art presents no economic difficulty—gives him an extraordinary freedom. It is not unreasonable to regard this as a dangerous freedom, seeing the uses to which it has been so often put in recent years. The restraints put on a creator whose medium is the cinematograph are so great that he may be said to have no freedom at all—which is a bad thing too. He can only make a film if it is satisfactory in the view of his public; which is of course why there are so few good films, and equally why there are no extreme ones.

Both cinema and theatre, at the present time, in the Anglo-Saxon countries, produce almost nothing but the most tiresome and vulgar plays, in part on account of this terrifying costliness of the material and of theatre rents. The theatre as much as the cinema suffers. It is necessary to mention this, but do not let us be confused by it. The opera and ballet, even more than the theatre, would suffer from this most tremendous handicap were it not for the subsidies which, at the present time, both enjoy.

IV

The Irresponsible Freedom of the Visual Artist

AT first sight the beautiful freedom of the painter appears to make his art potentially superior to any other. But in practice it is not quite like that. The nineteenth-century artist was lavishly paid for his work, 'art' being a valuable commodity. The last fifty years, however, has seen a steady decline in the value of a newly painted picture, and, since World War Two and the ensuing impoverishment, and with the coming of the welfare state, the virtual disappearance of the picture-buying rich-man, the collector of new pictures, the artist no longer has the temptation to grow rich. At the start of his career, he knows that what he paints has, as it were, no commercial value. There are various semi-charitable institutions, and now there are institutes, from which he can derive support if he pleases or impresses by his extremism. But there is nothing to be gained by painting a pleasant, a recognizable or comprehensible picture (unless he be so inferior an artist, and so unimaginative a man that the Royal Academy is, in fact, his natural home).

It would be thought, at first sight, that this was an ideal situation for the artist (provided he could keep alive). As it works out, however, it possesses a disadvantage of a very serious kind. Not measureless freedom, but a new and insidious compulsion is what results for the artist. This has been described as a 'new academy'. The public naturally find it difficult to understand this paradox. I will endeavour in the next few pages to provide the public with the information that is necessary: then it should be possible for them to appreciate how the artist may have imposed upon him *an obligation to be free*—which is not freedom.

20

V

The Cause of the Heterogeneity in the Fine Arts in Our Time

IF you go through the picture-galleries of Italy or of Germany where old masters are hung, ranged according to period, there is a great homogeneity in the paintings of each period, so that you know at once when you are among the canvases of such-and-such a school. This homogeneity of the works of any time, or school, continues up to French Impressionism. You then find yourself among painters so different as Manet and Monet, as Degas and Whistler (nocturnes). Within a few decades you reach Van Gogh, John Sargent, and Gauguin. A few decades more and you would be surrounded by Cubists, Futurists, religious pictures by Rouault and Augustus John. As you advanced from decade to decade the confusion, the lack of homogeneity would grow. In England today (1954) you would be among pure Impressionists like Coldstream, those who prefer carpentry to paint, like Passmore, traditionalists like Augustus John, Post-Impressionists like Trevelyan. We have reached a point at which there is not much money to be extracted from the painting of pictures, and artists pursue their fancies: so you find side by side painters of all sorts of schools. There is still a certain amount of mild excitement when a few people are under the impression that they are *des avant-gardes*, and still exhibit a little superiority about those who are not so far ahead as themselves. The I.C.A. provides them with a rallying ground.

Now, the proliferation of schools began with the bitter hostilities between the classicists and the romantics at the beginning of the nineteenth century. This was a war between the new and the old. The battle between the new and the old has continued up to the present moment. The only difference is that for a long time almost any group is denounced as 'old' at the end of about ten years of life. Since this group of noisy denouncers is in its turn denounced in a decade, or half a decade, or even twelve months—this has meant that very soon there were dozens of schools and groups claiming to be *le dernier cri*, the quintessence of revolution, so much the latest thing that they are almost out of sight, as are some of the dimmest of the Abstractists in post-war Paris.

This heterogeneity is not an explosion of rugged individualism, but, on the contrary, quite the opposite. The personality is surrendered to some small well-disciplined group: it is always as groups that they advance to the attack upon the obsolete. If the contemporary scene could be confined to any one of these groups, it would seem a very homogeneous period.

What is the explanation of this universal disunion? In the eighteenth and in the seventeenth centuries there was the homogeneity of discipline, the like-thinking of a classical norm. The turning-point was political; the age of political revolution was followed by the era of perpetual revolution in the arts. Halfway through the last century the revolutionary zest, the turmoil of schools, the roaring of slogans and watch-words began to assume a crazy intensity. But at present, halfway through the twentieth century, revolution, of a visual kind, appears to have become stabilized at a point which is as far as it is possible to go technically, without disappearing altogether—without the visual arts committing suicide. There are several abstract schools on the continent which the slightest push would tip over into the blankness of the great zero. It is my belief that we are approaching the point where there will be no visual arts at all, of a serious kind. On the one hand, the 'advanced' gestures, the project-foolery, will become stabilized; on the other hand, something like the Royal Academy will survive (unless there happened to be an authentic social revolution), trying to be a little vapidly go-ahead here and there, but still remaining a market-place for portraits of people who regard an oil-painting as a symbol of the sitter having arrived. Real whole-time painting, of the kind practised by the old masters, will not even pretend to exist any longer. This is not quite yet more than speculation.

All these pretentious little crusades, or gestures of revolution, certainly date from the period of the French Revolution at the end of the eighteenth century; although receiving their first impetus from a social revolution, the subsequent upheavals related purely to technical modifications. In the first decades of the last century painting, to start with, merely mirrored the mighty battle of the new and the old; so there was a grand cleavage into two schools of painting, the classicism of Ingres standing confronted by the romanticism of Delacroix or Géricault. A new factor becomes apparent after that: namely the invasion of the visual arts by the spirit of scientific discovery—the French painters were seized by the desire to make their imitation of nature more scientifically exact. They studied the theory of colour and this eventually led to the following system: (1) the colours were, as usual, squeezed out upon the palette; (2) the colours were not mixed with one another, neither on the palette nor on the canvas; small dabs of each colour were transferred intact from palette to canvas; (3) the theory was that the colours would mix in the eye of the spectator—they must never be allowed to mix anywhere else, but to preserve their original purity. The Pointillistes adhered most rigidly to this rule, and were the culmination of these experiments. A borrowing of a quite different kind from science, in the present century, was jeeringly named Cubism. So, from the middle of the last century, a pseudo-scientific impulse has been apt to start some school; reflected from science, there has been the impulse incessantly to perfect, constantly discarding what has been bettered, like yesterday's model in the motorcar industry; and last, but not least, the fiery millennial zeal of the social revolutionary emotionally galvanizing everything, and instilling the painter with a quite irrational belief in the *rightness* of his *latest* mannerism.

For the last hundred years the art-student has found himself
at the centre of a brawl between old and new, assailed by the
claims of schools or of leading artists to be ahead in the race,
or to possess some secret of technical up-to-dateness. When I
was an art-student in Paris in the first years of the century, it
was reported that leading artists, like Picasso, had passed into
a new 'period'. Picasso had begun his career with a 'blue period',
for instance. No student would be in the swim who did not
develop, himself, a green period, say, or a saffron one. To
eliminate from the palette all but one colour appeared to these
people the most easily recognized way of having a 'period'. I
can give you another illustration of what *period* means in the
life of the painter. Once a week, I think it was, a group of
painters formed the habit of meeting in the large first-floor
of 'The Newcomes' in Fitzroy Street, not long before World
War One. I remember, on one occasion, Walter Sickert dramatically announcing, in a rhyme which still rings in my ears:

> Mr. Ginner's
> Painting thinner.
> Mr. Sicker's
> Painting thicker.

This meant of course, that the painter, Charles Ginner, was
entering upon a 'thin period'; whereas Walter Sickert was
going thick—was having a 'thick period'.

The pictures of the more authentic masters of the past did
not suddenly develop curious rashes—you do not find Rem-
brandts or Titians of certain years all of a crude green or a
crude blue colour. But the mercurial masters of the budding
century had to give the student-mass a new sensation every
few years, or even, sometimes, if they felt they were losing
ground, every few months, by *going red*, or by *going blue*. Then
the students would follow suit and in the *Salon des Indépen-
dants* the fashionable colour would appear everywhere.

Let me return, now, to the question of the heterogeneity of
the arts in the modern age. We have not one manner, as in the

past, but dozens of ways of expressing ourselves. It will be obvious from this that the individuality of the artist is the last thing you are likely to find. Each artist conforms to one or other of the violent orthodoxies of the moment. Women are obedient to the annual fiats of fashion from Paris, and an artist has no more individuality than has a woman, whose only desire is to conform to the fashion. So when I speak of the freedom of the artist in my next section, it cannot mean that the artist is personally, or individually, free. That is not a thing that could possibly happen anywhere today.

VI

Amateur Artists

OURS is an age, inevitably, of amateurism in the fine arts: there are a countless number of people who are identified as artists, and most of them, even where they have had a little training, remain amateurs. Thirty years ago, for instance, while the middle-class still had money, 'art' was very often chosen as a career by a young man who had nothing in particular he wanted to do. It was an attractive way of doing nothing. It did not mean that any talent whatever was possessed by this young man; if he had told himself to start with that he had talent, he very soon found that he had been mistaken. These conditions were productive of a great number of what passed as professional artists. As the British Empire became a less and less attractive place to do nothing in (to be a soldier for instance), such a 'profession' as this became an obvious refuge. But this no longer could be regarded as a solution, I suppose, when the welfare state took over, and the middle-class family no longer had the money to pay for so expensive an education.

This accounts for quite a few of the amateurs technically professionals. Then, at the end of World War Two, upon demobilization (when the State stepped in, with a lavish financing) a number of young soldiers adopted the career of an artist. Quite apart from either of these two classes of artist, there is the enormous quantity of young men of all classes who find their way every year into provincial art-schools or into the Royal College of Art and other large metropolitan academies. There are, of course, nearly as many women as men studying to be some kind of artist. Talent is not often met with; but a great number of more or less youthful people are trained as artists: and it is from among this horde that the stunt crusades are recruited—the more violently untalented would no doubt soon drop out, if it were not for the opportunities offered the dud in extremism.

The army of technicians required by commercial art (which has turned the art-schools into a group of specialized classes, dressmaking, poster-art, or what not), this today is the most solid cause of the swarming of young men and women to which I have referred. But if there were, instead of these conditions, a small number of professional' artists, for the most part lucratively employed, then there would probably be no extremism. Extremism is symptomatic of a vacuum—a time in which there is no rationale for visual expression. It would be quite impossible to persuade any professional artist (at a time when such a profession was intact) to indulge in unpopular adventures.

For quite a time it has been so unwelcome to point out the realities of the present period that a sort of conspiracy of silence has developed. Everyone pretends, including the horde of impoverished artists, the professional pundits, the picture-dealers and so on, everyone pretends that we enjoy normal conditions, and even that art is flourishing. This is the necessary background for what I am shortly to examine—the institutional unreality, as also the costly 'cultural' bluffs inaugurated by the state, to conceal the growing absence of culture behind these imposing façades.

VII

Those who are Accessible to an Extremist Glamour

THE visual artist, alone in his studio, if of a technically inventive disposition, is easily tempted to go back and imagine himself a primitive, or to go forward into the future and imagine himself in a society far more intellectual, and sensitively receptive, than the one in which he finds himself. Then naturally, works will be produced which may seem very queer indeed to the public.

If technically a brilliant performer—as was, for instance, Pablo Picasso—the artist will be unwilling to abandon traditional achievement entirely. The great skills he has acquired it will give him delight to employ, and he will continue existing, to some extent, upon the plane of Leonardo or of El Greco, he will have a dual personality. In the case of Picasso, we find him producing, side by side, works as abstract as a coloured rug, and others quite naturalistic, if strongly marked with his personal idiosyncrasies. Otherwise, if there is no inducement of that kind to cling to naturalistic form and colour, if the artist's power is very moderate, an artist may use his paint and brush, or his chisel, to create forms and combinations reminiscent of the rough sketches of the engineer and the carpenter rather than the artist; indulge himself in 'advances' which are so far removed from normal sensuous experience as to alienate him entirely from any possible public, except, in such a time as ours, the snobbish patron or pundit, not necessarily an intelligent or sensitive man, who cares to spend his life among very strange images indeed. But the readiness on the part of an artist to step over into a type of fanciful engineering is usually due to the fact that the visual arts have no

very great attraction for him, he has no roots in the sensuous
reality, or he would not be willing to desert them. Whatever
he did in the way of experiment (and let us remember that the
word *experiment* is the word used to account for these depar-
tures from the practice of visual art that we inherit from all
past ages, whether Greek, Far-Eastern, or Italian Renaissance),
that experiment would be within the regions of visual sensibility
—never outside them.

It is all a question of whether the individual artist is one of
those rare ones who are greatly gifted, and if he has acquired,
in the course of a long training, a great deal of traditional
power; in a case of that kind there would be no chance that he
would allow himself to be dragged off into the problematical
wilderness of the future. He would be too satisfied to find himself where he was, to listen to the aesthetic excursionist. It is
unimaginable that the man who painted the portrait of Thomas
Carlyle and that of Miss Alexander, were he today of vigorous
middle age, would break up his perfection, and launch out
into the abstract. With a young man, not yet fully trained, it
is another matter. If the glorious reality of his gifts is not yet
visible, present to his eyes, he might do anything. Nevertheless, it is usually those of very little talent who furnish the
little crowds of people painting empty abstractions, or sticking together lengths of heavy iron, or platinum, or tin, which
goes under the name of sculpture.

VIII

There is a Limit, beyond which there is Nothing

I AM writing this not long after the death of Stalin, and there is a general feeling that, perhaps, the new rulers of Russia are going to modify the aggressive policy of the old leader. For the time being to speak of a third world war would be unpopular, but it still, unfortunately, is something which might happen at any moment. In the case of a third disaster of this kind, and one of unspeakable 'totality', the position of the fine arts, and the other great civilized forms of expression, would be profoundly changed, if the arts did not disappear altogether. So anything one says about the future is provisional: and anything one says about the present must have a certain unreality because of the 'cold war', which dislocates our national economies, and always has implicit in it the hottest war yet.

Having made this necessary statement, let me proceed. In the last section I spoke of Picasso's great traditional power, in painting and drawing, which he acquired when he was young. That was a period over fifty years ago; it was a time when Europe was at peace, and when it was possible laboriously to prepare for the career of a painter in a society unable even to imagine impoverishment, disposed to patronize all the arts and to spend considerable sums of money at the picture dealers and at the annual exhibitions. How vastly different that was from the present time goes without saying: all one need say is that an art student had leisure to build up the technical abilities which he required. Does he enjoy those conditions today? He certainly does not, and that solid mastery is not to be looked for in a time like the present. Artists are able to conceal the fact that this power is not possessed by them: to become an extremist of the most irrational stamp is one of the most obvious ways. Eighty years ago French impressionism offered a concealment of the same kind for the incompetent; but it was not a tenth as good a means of evasion as that provided by the arid bluff of *Réalités Nouvelles*, and all similar extremism.

Now, if you will consider the case of a young Englishman of eighteen or nineteen today, who feels he has an aptitude for painting; if, with me, you will examine the influences shaping his young mind, I believe you will find out a great deal about the position of the fine arts at the present moment. First of all, he will have visited the dealers' galleries, the R.A., have read the contemporary art journalism, possibly have gone to Paris. If he is a bright young man, he will imagine himself in the future an extremist: youth is always attracted by extremism. But it is not only that. What else is there for a bright young man to imagine himself? *There is no painting today worthy of consideration between extremist painting and the Royal Academy.* This is the essential fact that you must try to understand if you want to put yourself *au courant*. So a long traditional training would be the last thing he would think about. The fact that Reg Butler received four thousand five hundred pounds [1] would be an enormous advertisement for extremism, suggesting to the bright young man that *even economically* extremism was a good bet. So there would not be much likelihood that he would do more than learn how to be a very extreme painter, or a frightfully advanced sculptor.

What is being done in England on a small scale, is being done in France in a big way. If you go to Paris and try to find a painter not an extremist, and not the French equivalent of the Royal Academy—one who is highly thought of—you will be disappointed. There is no such painter. There is a rash of total abstraction, and of near-abstraction. Under these

[1] Cf. Section X.

circumstances, it is safe to assume that in France the bright young man will think the same thoughts as the bright young man in England.

What does this mean? It means, I think, that there will be no more artists (painters or sculptors) possessing the great traditional accomplishment which is possessed by Pablo Picasso, or, in this country, Augustus John or Jacob Epstein may be cited as possessing, or, to take an advanced artist, Henry Moore.

I will end this section by saying that, as far as I personally am concerned, I do not object to the extremism of Henry Moore or of Graham Sutherland. In my own work I pushed at all times to that limit, although doing fairly traditional work as well. Having made this statement, let me add that extremism is not *necessary*. It is all right; some people tend to be extremist, and some are not extremist. There is no merit in extremism: although at the present moment it is a universal fashion. What I am arguing about in this book is that an easily defined limit exists in painting and sculpture, in music, in the theatre, in literature, in architecture, and in every other human art. There are daring drivers who enjoy driving along the edge of a cliff, whenever the opportunity offers. All I am saying is that there is such a thing as driving *too near* the edge of a cliff. There is no sense in shooting over it. It is quite simple; beyond a certain well-defined line—in the arts as in everything else—beyond that limit there is *nothing*. Nothing, zero, is what logically you reach past a line, of some kind, laid down by nature, everywhere.

As you must understand, we have reached the point at which a quite final position has to be taken up. It is where you have to say *yes* or *no*.

Because of its intricacy, and because, in the second place, I run the risk of putting in danger the effectiveness of my general line of argument, what I now have to say is particularly difficult.

Infantile extremist sensationalism (as a by-product of self-seeking) is the curse of the pundit. What every artist should try to prevent is the car, in which is our civilized life, plunging over the side of the precipice—the exhibitionist extremist promoter driving the whole bag of tricks into a nihilistic nothingness or zero.

Great — but one cannot stop the world from flow. We are headed "naturally" toward nihilism, in the same way that we headed toward the Renaissance in the 12th century. I value your great concern, however, & deeply appreciate your recognition of the end — or of a beginning. Man cannot prevent the rotting of a corpse! Not yet!

IX

The Ability to See the Limit

OVER thirty years ago I was teaching extremism, and I was myself an extreme artist. The extremist modes in European painting and sculpture of that time have not been exceeded, for the very good reason that there is no way of exceeding (developing a more spectacular extremism) Mondrian's geometric frames, Brancusi's eggs, or Kandinsky's atmospheric inventions or explosions. I have mentioned Henry Moore and Graham Sutherland as artists of the extreme whose adventures I do not look upon with a critical eye. Here is the great difficulty in such an anti-extremist argument as I am developing in this study. The trouble is, of course, that the extremism of Moore and Sutherland appears excessive to the majority of people; and my own work has offended, in the past, by its unorthodox character. The objection that will be made is that an extremist cannot be allowed to say, 'So far, but no farther!' It is quite arbitrary, fanciful, and irrational—so it must seem—this line beyond which there must be no advance.

Now the difficulty really is that no one not an artist can ever in fact *see* this line. He does not know enough about these matters to understand how, once you have accepted something described as 'extremism', there can ever be a *limit*. If a painter uses his thumb as a palette knife, and, jabbing it into various colours upon his palette, rubs them one after the other upon a blank canvas, and sends this 'picture' to the *Réalités Nouvelles* exhibition in Paris, that logically should be acceptable to anyone describable as an extremist. This is the conundrum which I have to tackle.

Now I must ask you to believe that I see the line beyond

which the extreme is the nonsensical. But in any such discussion, those who are not painters will have to take a good deal on trust—simply because they cannot see what differentiates a highly logical piece of 'extremism' of Picasso's from an average work hung in the *Réalités Nouvelles* exhibitions. However, I hope you will continue with me, and much later in these pages I will make a final attempt to overcome this obstacle to comprehension.

X

'The Unknown Political Prisoner' and After

IN England, the last example of militant extremism was the
collection of works at the Tate Gallery, representing 'The
Unknown Political Prisoner'. A touch of the old excitement
was conjured up: first of all a prize was given, to the young
sculptor, Reg Butler, of the most sensational kind, namely
four thousand five hundred pounds. This small model of a pro-
posed monument upon the white Cliffs of Dover appeared a
very insignificant piece of eccentricity to those who had been
reading in the papers, with amazement, of the vast sum it had
gained for its creator. All the newspapers contained a photograph of this oddity. Then came the second sensation: a young
Hungarian went to the Tate, and, seizing this little joke by
its spine of wire, doubled it up and threw it on the floor.
As a result of this demonstration the young Hungarian
spent some time in gaol, lost his job, and at last the case was
dismissed.

Because of these well-advertized events, Reg Butler became,
for the public, a symbol of outrageous 'advancedness'. But
this intellectual toy of his is not at all a novelty, since many
thousands of similar things have been produced, over and over
again, for the last thirty or forty years in every part of Europe
and America.

Let me here make use of Reg Butler's name, then, as it will
be familiar to most people. The interested spectator of these
goings-on will no doubt enjoy a pleasurable expectation of
what next will happen in this funny old game the artists keep
on playing.

So, what next? Well, there is nothing much beyond this

simple little stunt—that is the odd thing. The same thing, more or less, has served to focus the popular mind for a long time now. There is nothing new to be expected; we shall, I assume, see Reg Butlers and the fanatical sterilities of *Réalités Nouvelles* for a long time to come; for, as a matter of fact, the advances of the last forty years have about reached the limits of the visual. There is not much more that can be done in senseless progress.

In the end, of course, the pundits will be shamed out of stopping at Reg Butler. Someone will invent something or other which will *seem* a new departure. What ultimately must be expected is that a step will be taken outside or beyond nature. They will not be in a hurry to take this step—for it is a much better bet for these gentlemen to keep on marking time, as long as people will stand it, in the same spot more or less. For if they take Art over the edge, what will happen to *them*? But they are really so irresponsible, and probably have not thought out all this. So it is incumbent upon everybody to halt them here and now.

So there is no tomorrow, there is no *new* sensation to be expected. The rational limit has already been overstepped—there is nothing more to be anticipated. Indeed, what has been reached is hardening into a canon, behind which everything is described as bad.

All artists today, and art-critics, are familiar with what a painting, or a piece of sculpture, looks like when it has reached the *ne plus ultra* line. For thirty years, we all have become sickeningly familiar with these formulae. Even originality-in-extremeness is not encouraged: the new extremists must reproduce what is there already, what has been done many times before. You would think that that sickening feeling of which I have spoken would be felt by the newcomer, the young extremist, just as much as by everyone else. The curious thing is that he seems to think he is being wildly 'advanced' when he is reproducing, in reality, something done for the first time thirty or forty years ago. But there it is; there are certain set

ways of doing things, it has all been laid down some time
ago in the Anglo-Saxon countries. The young artist, when, at
whatever point in his progress, he decides to go abstract, has a
rigid and fixed number of directions he can take. All he can do
is to pick such and such a well-trodden approach to zero, and,
then, within that well-trodden approach to the Great Blank,
he can indulge in a few· minor and insignificant variations.
Or, shall we say that he is like a performing white mouse entering a carefully defined and ingeniously worked out maze. No
originality is possible any longer; what he paints or what he
carves must look very much like thousands of other things
we all have seen. The only original artist was he who pioneered
in this elaborate game; who blazed the trail, marked out the
paths to be taken, and reached the limit beyond which it was
impossible to go. He was like the man who discovered the
Pacific, 'silent upon a peak in Darien'. Well, there is only one
Pacific. Once you have discovered the Pacific you can draw a
map of this region, and show how other people can come and
discover the Pacific too. After that, naturally, there is the
Pacific to cross, its islands must be charted, the shores of
Australia and of Asia reached; and from there you just, stage
by stage, come back to where you began, to the point from
which you set out. All 'advancedness', in this kind of advancedness, is merely a repetition of this circumnavigation. The earth
is round, and, in the technical 'advance' in the fine arts
initiated in the second decade of this century, it is a question
merely of going round and round. The young artist soon, now,
reaches the 'peak in Darien'. Then, without having to be a
very daring fellow, he crosses the Pacific; he reaches the Spice
Islands and Asia; from there is a journey home that seems as
old as the camel-route across Asia. To perform this journey
the ingenious Calder has provided you with all the wire you
will need, if you are travelling in the third dimension; Picasso
and Braque, and hundreds of other initiators, have hammered
away billions of models required by the Abstractist, from
which you select if you are a painter. This is hard tack, or it

may be thought of as pemmican, but anyway it is all the young 'adventurer' will need in his journey.

Now, the painter 'travels light', as I have pointed out. The material he needs to be a painter costs him practically nothing. Theoretically his freedom should be very great. But as an 'advanced', Abstractist, painter or sculptor in our time, his *freedom* is merely theoretic, his originality nil. Everyone has been original before him. He is handed a guidebook, a set of rules, a lot of 'uplift'. He has to paint as he is told, he has to register his adherence to the laws of advance. What he eventually turns out must conform to what is by this time a well-tried formula.

Apart from the pundits, like Herbert Read, who provide books of 'advanced' theory, there are naturally, a great number of instructors in the art-schools (like the Central, the R.C.A., etc., in London, and similar places in all the large provincial cities) who can teach any student how to become an 'advanced' artist. These teachers can provide all the formulae of painting of the *Réalités Nouvelles* type, or of sculpture of the Reg Butler type; or, if 'mobiles' attract, it can be shown how this is done. If some kind of infantilism is what the student appears to be marked out for, encouragement and instruction are supplied. It is just the same as in the days of Frith, when students were given instruction, after they had gone through the preliminaries, in how to paint a 'Derby Day'. Thirty or forty years ago there were instructors in art-schools who would put a student on the road to produce a typical Van Gogh 'Sunflower'; but this is *vieux jeu*, literally, almost as much so as the 'Derby Day', for Van Gogh was nowhere near the limit of technical 'advance'.

Near the limit of technical advance—the Twentieth Century front line.

XI

The 'Progressive' Slave

THE other day I was talking to one of those extremist painters whose work I greatly like. In the course of our conversation I was somewhat surprised to hear him speak as follows. 'It is strange,' he observed, 'but we have to struggle just as hard today to do something . . . well, like painting a recognizable portrait . . . as formerly we had for years to struggle to be allowed to do something "extremist" or whatever you like to call it. Today it is just the same thing the other way round. One's dealer raises his eyebrows, frowns upon a more or less straight portrait when one sends it in. It has become like a religious orthodoxy. Yet, when we began to depart from the traditional norm, it was not a departure that had anything religious about it—it was not a catholic doing something anti-catholic. It was just a desire to experiment in the medium one was using, no more than that, was it?'

I was delighted to learn that even the most successful extremist (of the rational kind) did not find it necessary to conceal the difficulty he encountered in defying the canon of advancedness. Under similar circumstances I am quite sure, of course, that Pablo Picasso did not have to ask permission of his dealer to paint a portrait, of a naturalistic kind. But then he had attained, long ago, to such a pinnacle of worldly success that to him all was permitted. To the rank and file extremist *nothing* is permitted. He is a slave of the great god Progress, who is a very jealous god indeed.

Part II

THE PAINTING ANIMAL AND THE PUNDIT

XII

The Painting Animal

THE public for the visual arts is (i) that part of any cultivated society specially interested in the visual arts; and
(2) the more numerous body of people who form the public for
every art, but with no especial leaning for one art more than
the other. In both of these publics some quite erroneous ideas
prevail as to what goes on behind the scenes; they see the
painting or the sculpture, but that is all they know about it.
What makes the painter tick, as the late Mr. Roosevelt would
have put it, is hidden from them. Of the way pictures are produced they have the haziest notion; what picture dealers are
like, or what newspaper art-critics are like, they know no more
than the personal appearance of the dealer who walks about
in a gallery where pictures are being exhibited in one of the
dozen picture shops. Since one of the functions of this book is
to help the public to understand pictures, and since, in order to
do this it would be of the greatest use to understand, first of
all, the man who paints them, I will attempt to throw some
light upon the painter's mentality. There is one feature of this
which is of first-rate importance for the outside world to know.
I have never seen this explained to the public, and regard it
as a serious omission on the part of those who spend their time
in acting as self-appointed guides.

Perhaps the first thing to remember about the artist, then,
is that it is quite essential that he should begin his training
at an early age. If he does not do this, then it is rather as if the
ordinary learning of a school and university had to be started
at the age when men normally graduate. It would of course
be intensely difficult to start your schooling at the age of
twenty-two. It could, I suppose, be done, but a man so unfor-
tunate as to have to do this would be called upon to make a

quite unnatural effort. It is really just the same with a painter
who enters an art-school at that age, and very few successful
painters have done so.

Well then, as schoolboys they begin learning how to draw
and paint, instead of studying history and algebra, Latin and
French. As to philosophy, higher mathematics and things like
that, which are studied before the university is reached, they
miss that level of ordinary learning. Add to this the fact that
most painters have always come from working-class families,
it is not surprising that they are ill-equipped to cope with the
pundit, or the man of letters who comes over into their field
and proceeds to teach them their own business.

The painter has a tendency to regard himself as somewhat of a 'dumb ox', as a *painting animal*. The painter will
relish enormously the life of Cézanne by that master's dealer,
Vollard. It is really a very admirable biography, and intensely
amusing—amusing at the expense, of course, of Cézanne, who
was a perfect 'dumb animal'. Vollard's account of him makes
it quite clear that Cézanne fully understood the position—
knew that he was a divine idiot, and that he greatly resented
those men, trained in universities, who meddled with his craft.
Whenever the word 'professor' was uttered, Cézanne would fly
into a rage. If this occurred at mealtimes, the master would
exclaim violently 'Ah, les professeurs!', spring up, and leave
the table. He objected to *all* professors, since he had met
several whose goings-on almost drove him mad. He was a case
of a painter who resisted the inroads of the man of letters, but
knew it was no good, and that his hatred was unavailing
against the word-man.

So Cézanne was an instinctive, and that is something which
is aggressively prized by the typical painter. To arrive, by
some intuitive process, at his great technical discoveries, at
his remarkable innovations, rather as the peasant-mystic
arrives at his religious intuitions, that is an order of things
very much favoured by many painters (who, on the whole,
could not arrive at anything in any other way). Perhaps they

are conscious of their own cultural limitations, owing to the necessity of having to acquire their training in the techniques of their craft at an age which precludes the acquisition of any of those useful things which lift a man above the helpless level of the labourer.

But it is not only that; the fact is that painting and sculpture are things which can only be known *à fond* by a man trained as a painter; so painters feel themselves locked up in this mystery, in this knowledge, this secret craft. They have, and quite rightly, a contempt for any opinion about a picture by people who have not been trained as painters; for it *is* a mystery, and it is ultimately painters who settle the values of pictures—who dictate whether they are masterpieces or not. The critic knows quite well that his judgement cannot be final, that it has to be taken to some painter, or sculptor (naturally the one considered by him the most gifted—however idiotic), it has to be laid before him, and if it is not accepted by the artist, there is an end of the matter.

All painters, the most mediocre, understand this situation very well, and can look the critic haughtily in the eye, and cause him to feel his place, if he does not know it already. All those who paint regard the painter of genius with awe, as a man who has, in the highest degree, the mastery of the secret. They rejoice, with exultation, at the farcical stories, such as those of Monsieur Vollard, about their hero, showing what a dumb, stupid, if you like, creature he was. For he was not as other men; he was a heaven-sent idiot, the essential painter, and nothing else. He was not a man, he was a painter.

In every high craft a consciousness of isolation, similar to this, exists. More than in any other, I suppose, there is in higher mathematics a sense of apartness conjoined with superiority. The mathematician is a man who, in his highest flights of imagination, is familiar with realities so augustly remote from the daily round of human life, and is the master of a craft as inaccessible as painting or sculpture, that he must regard himself, to some extent, as privileged among men as is the artist. Also, all those occupied in the most abstruse mathematical fields are bound to experience a sensation of electness, and can hardly escape twinges of superiority—and with much more justification than any but the greatest artist.

But there is no craft so humble but the craftsman derives a certain satisfaction in knowing that there is no man alive (not of his craft) who can do what he can do, whether it be a piece of fine cabinet-making, or the growing in a hot-house of a rare plant.

This craft-mysticism is a very important thing to know about, for those outsiders who have never painted pictures, but who interest themselves in them, and wish for a little more competence than merely those who say 'I know what I like'. A real grasp of this situation (for it deserves the name of *situation*) is enormously valuable to a person trying to understand the inner workings of the visual arts in our time. It takes a rather different form today, but it has always existed; for the painter and sculptor have always been confronted by the same difficulty, that to do a thing *well*, the way they wanted to do it, and felt that it should be done, was not the way that would be most satisfactory to the patron or to the public. There must always have been among these craftsmen a feeling—indeed, a knowledge—that only they were capable of judging their work; of giving an opinion as to whether a piece of work was good, bad, or indifferent. I am sure that the people that they had to deal with, three or four hundred years ago, were not only far more accommodating, but far better able to understand. The senses of those earlier publics had not been vulgarized and demoralized, as ours have, by camera and a hundred other devices. Also mass-life today is the worst kind of thing for an appreciation of the arts, or of any cultural product. One must go much farther than this, however. The absurd things which are happening in the visual arts at present are what must happen when an art becomes almost totally disconnected from society, when it no longer has any direct function in life, and can only exist as the plaything of the intellect.

XIII

The Pundit-Prophet

NOW that I have given the general reader some idea of this strange being who lives for painting, wrapt away at the heart of an inaccessible universe of values not shared by the rest of the world—now that you know something of the mind of this animal whose carvings or whose pictures you go and look at, let me turn to another figure, namely the pundit who has recently promoted himself 'art historian', but who is more generally known as art-critic.

This, at its most energetic, is a figure of the utmost importance in the art world; and as he battens parasitically upon that painting animal I have just been describing, and in one way or another (even more, perhaps than the dealer) affects his destiny, he merits immediate attention.

First of all, this is a word-man. He is a writer, usually attempting, to begin with, to be a poet, a philosopher, a fiction-writer, or what not; but not succeeding in any of these directions, he goes and lives with the artist: rather in the way that a man who is not getting on very well at home, emigrates.

One must consider, at this point, how different the literary world is from the art world. The life-form of a book is starkly dissimilar from that of an oil-painting or a piece of sculpture. The visual arts and literature differ profoundly physically and that involves a great difference in the way literature reacts to the influences of the time. Words are more powerful than images; they have the advantage of the civilized man over the primitive man. There is that. And so, naturally, a book can look after itself a great deal better than can an oil-painting, and a writer can look after himself far better than can a painter, because, to start with, he knows a great deal more. If you remember this simple fact, you will understand how it is possible for the writer to come over among the painters and to make of the products of the painter's art his specialization. He dazzles this ignorant craftsman with his words. When he has learned enough about painting, by carefully listening to what his painter friends say about it, listening in to their disputes, and when he has absorbed enough of the literary work, tons of which collects around modern painting, he writes a book.

One may simplify this story, and say that a book has come over among a lot of paintings, and eventually climbs on their backs, and perhaps runs away with them. But the functions of the book and of the painting are quite different. For so it is; a painting cannot go over among the books, climb on their backs, mesmerize them and misdirect them, and stampede them in this direction or that. A book, however, can very easily do this with paintings. So a book may be parasitic, it may inflame a thousand paintings and lead them off to the moon, or anywhere else it fancies. But I should not have said it fancies; for these technical crusades which get the painter's creations whirled off to some remote no man's land, are initiated among painters and, in the first instance, are concerned purely with questions deriving from the artist's material, the problems of the painter's art. But when adopted by a man of letters, this will become a slightly different crusade. It may for instance, by its absolutist tone, by its irrational fervour, appear rather as the crusade of a religionist or of a millennial politician.

The writer may be thought of as a Viking, as a man of prey —though, Heaven knows, the specimens of this Viking that we meet with are usually hardly impressive enough to live up to so fiercely predatory a name. The painter, by the way, would be inclined to laugh at this analysis of what happens to him, for he may be conceited as well as ignorant; but I can vouch for its accuracy.

When I see a writer, a word-man, among a number of painters, I shake my head. For I know that he would not be there unless he was up to something. And I know that he will do them no good; but the reverse. When I was young I was approached by these pirates; but when they found that I was an *intelligent* painter, they moved away. I was never popular with the pundit. My encounter with Mr. Roger Fry was an excellent example.

But I have no intention of calling myself in as a witness. And there are exceptions to what I have said of the predatory pundit: I think of John Ruskin, who was not only a very great writer, who had a remarkable influence upon the prose style of his contemporaries, and who was so many-sided a man as to have astonished later economists by his originality, but who, by his prophetic activities in the field of art, was a benefactor.

The books of Ruskin were holy writ for several generations of painters. And in this age of crusades there is always some writer attempting, successfully or not, to occupy this rôle, —wonderfully eloquent like Ruskin, a great user of words, or just a journalist, a pedestrian prophet, it is all one. There must be some such writer there at hand.

In the last century John Ruskin was the most outstanding example of the literary man who goes over and lives with the artists, stimulates their activity, interprets them to the rest of the world, and, in a word, exploits the visual arts as I have described. Ruskin did more than this, and himself painted, in a limited way. Though he is the archetype of this kind of man he nevertheless is in a very different class from those writers who, in the present century, belong to the same group in literary history—the writers whose subject-matter is the visual arts in violent evolution.

There was, first of all, Roger Fry, the prophet of Post-Impressionism, a term invented by him. He possessed a considerable literary gift, and his books have an eloquence and grace which elevate them above the average of writers of this *genre*. Sir Kenneth Clark, who was Fry's literary executor, in a mild way followed in his footsteps, without however offering himself as a prophet. Sir Herbert Read is the most recent writer of this class. He is the pedestrian sorcerer, a Mister Abreast-of-the-Times for Everyman who paints or sculpts; he is the writer who has led the Salvation Army into a Promised Land, into an Institute. And, if you will tolerate any more imagery of this kind, he has done his best to lure Mammon into this tabernacle.

In the foregoing pages I have, I hope, introduced you to a novel figure, of whose real nature you had, up to now, no conception. But I am only able to speak very briefly of all these central figures in the art drama, who, each of them, play a part which is surprisingly unlike what is supposed to be their rôle by anyone who has not had access to life behind the scenes. Fully to substantiate my view of these goings-on I should have to write about all these people in much greater detail. All I can say is that I am sure that anyone penetrating to the intimacies of the art-life would, after a very short time, bear me out. He would soon encounter, I expect, the pundit-prophet of my recent descriptions—encouraging, or inflaming the waverer, supplying him with arguments, and luring him on to pursue the visual path towards an abstraction so stern as to resemble zero, or to be its brother in emptiness. This is the contemporary P.P.: he possesses no eloquence, but he has, in place of that, a kind of naïve persistence, a dogged conviction that the road to near zero is *the right road*. This is the contemporary type.

Explanatory Note on the Plates

OF the six illustrations, only two (numbers 1 and 2) are designed to illustrate the terrible pictorial aberration whose idiot name Real cannot be tolerated outside of the pathologic clinic. These are the only two photographs I have been able to obtain, owing to the death, this year, 1953–4, of the man apparently responsible for the promotion in Paris of the *Réalités Nouvelles* exhibitions. I wish I could have marshalled a few more; but it matters less than it would had any other type of picture been involved, since there is a deadly monotony about all 'New Real' canvasses. The 'New Real' dogma imposes this terrible sameness, just as the Mohammedan religion restricts the visual arts of Islamic countries to a lifeless monotony. What you see in numbers 1 and 2 is depressingly like any other *Réalités Nouvelles* pictures.

The other four pictures, 3, 4, 5 and 6 (between pages 58–59), are works of an opposite kind—belonging to the sort of painting that *Réalités Nouvelles* seeks to supersede—of the same pictorial order as the pictures to be seen in all our Galleries from the Roman heads and from Cimabue down to Augustus John and Pablo Picasso.

Mr. Francis Bacon's picture, number 4, may seem to the uninitiated not to belong to the traditional order. This, of course, would show how greatly the prospective reader was in need of the instruction contained in this book; for I cannot believe that after reading these pages it would be possible to make such a mistake. The fact is that the *Caprichos* of Goya and pictures by the Flemish artist Hieronymus Bosch, are very like the grotesqueries of Francis Bacon. Also, the ethical and literary impulses throughout the work of Bacon constitute him an artist at the opposite pole to the pretentious blanks and voids of *Réalités Nouvelles*.

The splendid portrait of Sir William Walton, by Michael Ayrton (number 3), would take its place anywhere in a collection of great historic portraits; the stylistic idiosyncrasy, identifying it as belonging to our time, is made a happy use of. The symbolic power of John Minton's picture (number 6) requires no comment; and the early portrait by Colquhoun (number 5) shows well the powerful formalizing character of the work of this very gifted young artist. These are only a few of the many fine contemporary English pictures from which it was possible for me to select. What the reader should understand is that these four pictures are all of them styled 'progressive' and 'modernistic'; but in order to make them *more so*—for them to 'advance' *still further*—there would be no sense in their 'advancing' into the nothingness and nullity of the 'New Real'.

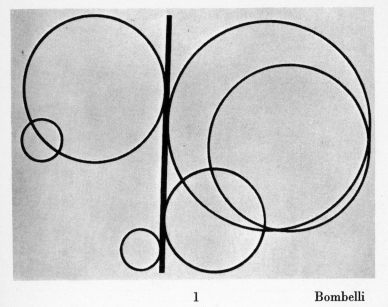

1   Bombelli

2   Engel-Pak

XIV

When the Painter is least Free

IT is a great mistake to think of the painter as free. He
could be free, to a certain extent, but he is not. His most
harebrained 'experiments' are not wild and daring acts of free
adventure; on the contrary, he is probably least free when most
eccentric. One has to think of him as a figurine in a ballet,
advancing with an identical élan, with a score of men exactly
like himself, in a studied rush.

No, the painter is pushed along paths which are not necessarily his paths, and all artists today submit to a will which is
not necessarily theirs. They have their programme of work
presented to them (as though they were performers in a highly
eccentric ballet) by a man who is not himself an artist, but a
theoretician who has not that love for the medium, the
material, *la matière*, which we find in the born artist. It is this
love for the material which anchors the artist, in some ways
and to some extent, in a manner unknown to the theoretician.
In the case of a master-artist, there is no question of his aban-
doning the delights of the material, and going to make scare-
crows in the wilderness; and with any man who is an authentic
painter, or sculptor in a lesser degree, the same repugnance for
the purely abstract obtains—I mean for absolute, as it were
islamic, shunning of the natural.

To be specific, whoever is able to create upon a canvas or a
piece of paper a human figure containing the reality of life,
or in stone or clay, or to bring into the world the vital reflec-
tion of a farm-yard, a ship's deck, a lake in the mountains, or
a storm at sea, is not likely to go off and satisfy himself by
drawing with a ruler a lot of strips upon a canvas or paper,
filling them in with colour, or producing a number of squares

51

and circles or a few triangles filled in with white or blue, or
mixing these things together. That would be like a man,
accustomed to the warmth and variety of the world outside,
going and shutting himself up in a bare stone or concrete cell.
Only a profoundly austere religionist would want to do that.
Visual abstraction is like a form of suicide, or a form of rigid
personal seclusion, or an isolation from life like the existence
of the Trappist monk.

Again, however, it may be recalled, I showed how even
the greatest artist born today would never be given time to
develop his powers; as for instance Picasso was able to. But
had he had this opportunity, and become a sort of magician,
he would never be likely to throw away his wand.

One of my principal objections to the pundit-prophet is that
he is always an agent of the *Zeitgeist*, whose function it is to
'inspire' (to drill and to discipline) a generation. The *Zeitgeist*
means fashion; and I do not think that the best work is done
when the compulsion of fashion is at its intensest. The fact
that this pundit has first to learn all his tricks from the painter,
and then to dragoon him according to a theory which is often
independent of painting, is an unsatisfactory situation. The
pundit has interests of his own and is apt to look at things
fundamentally differently from the painter, or sculptor, or
other visual artist. Often he knows very little about the craft
of painting. So, as an interpreter, he is not to be trusted. The
picture dealer is apt to know more about painting than does
the 'critic'. But there are times, nevertheless, when the pundit
has his uses: even if it is only to regularize an absurdity—or
to be responsible for a good funeral.

XV

The English Way

THE State bestows its legendary chivalrous honorific upon somebody who stands the human intelligence upon its head and, with a solemn frown, addresses his remarks to its footwear. This is a paradox such as is met with by Alice in the reverse regions the other side of the Looking Glass; and the State is to be congratulated for honouring something so divorced from vulgar common sense. And this is not irony. No other nation, as we know, enjoys such things as the Mad Hatter's tea party; and here is yet another illustration of how the English find Alice, and all her kind, irresistible as a model and exemplar. In Sir Herbert Read we have a man who has been very recently knighted for being so 'contemporary'; for having been for years ready to plug to the hilt, to trumpet, to expound, any movement in painting or sculpture—sometimes of the most contradictory kind—which was obviously hurrying along a path as opposite as possible from what had appealed to civilized man through the ages. This is a story of the *snobisme* of the advanced. The definition of the 'contemporary' for this distinguished pundit has been *the farthest possible from anything that has been seen before.* Accepting this definition, a man would be assured of contemporaneity who was highly uncontemporary with practically everyone alive.

Crowning this career, was the securing of the institutionalization of what is intellectualized beyond the sensuous regions of the fine arts, by the foundation of an institution, to be an anchorage for projects aimed at attaining to some metaphysical reality, after dismissing all of nature except the linear dream of a two-dimensional, white-blooded centipede. The institute to which I refer is, of course, 'The Institute of Contemporary Arts'—quite a small affair, but, for reasons I shall indicate, it does not have to be very large: only firmly cemented into its fairly expensive site. It is, as you see, named an institution, and also it is necessary to note that it is called 'contemporary'. It is an institute for the *contemporary*: the 'contemporary' being somewhere in the future, so far away as to be very remote from the present.

Money has been poured out in order to make this institution a reality. The State has smiled upon this budding institution and always been ready to help with what is public money. But the dream was Sir Herbert's. As a matter of fact, what Sir Herbert dreamed of to begin with was a museum of modern art; what he got was the institute of which he is president.

An institute is really much more rational than a museum. A 'museum', for such a purpose, can only be described as a hoax; whereas an 'institute', as interpreted in Dover Street, is airy enough to satisfy the insubstantial conditions of the time. It is very accurately in conformity with the floaty character of the *Zeitgeist*. Let us take, for instance, the last 'institutional' manifestation of the I.C.A. Eleven thousand pounds, distributed in a gallery lent by the Tate for a number of projects, is better than a 'museum', with thousands of projects masquerading as works of art. Metaphorically speaking, this sculpture exhibition, in the Tate Gallery, may be regarded as a kite. Here we become conscious of nationality. The English way to deal with this intellectual extremism, in an unintellectualized world, is to humour it, to leave it all floating in the air like a mysterious kite, anchored to an institution (which is, not a bogus, but a metaphysical institution) to the creation of which the state has contributed; into whose modest coffers whoever wishes to may throw a cheque for a thousand pounds or two—or eleven if he likes—and so a vaporous emanation of the institute, which I have called a kite, floats for a while in that airy art-palace, the Tate.

XVI

The American Way

THE American way is not to humour, but to take very seriously, this pioneering in an abstract future: to build an enormous museum in the centre of a major city, to purchase for it anything that anyone likes to *project* (with strips of wire, bits of tin, aluminum, slate, plastic, wood, or which is 'projected' in paint upon a canvas, or a lump of stone with some bits of wire protruding from it): and to pretend that this is a rarely significant work of art to preserve for future ages, something like the pictures of Leonardo, Signorelli, El Greco or Van Eyck.

Centuries hence (I fear it will not be before) someone will burst out laughing at this museum, like the child and the naked king in the fairy tale. *Taking literally* is the American way: building massive walls around a hazy idea; enshrining on granite foundations a little squinting image of zero.

Needless to say the English way is absurd, most absurd, *too*. But it is essential to realize that everything in life is absurd, and eleven thousand pounds or eleven billion pounds is the same thing: in art eleven *thousand* is what we get; in politics eleven *billion*. The only thing that is not absurd is what is found where the earth conditions are stable and peaceful enough to allow of the production of such great classical works as those of Leonardo, Michelangelo, Van Eyck, El Greco.

In England we will, I feel sure, be sufficiently mature at no time *to collect for posterity* a quantity of bric-à-brac, of childishly pretentious shorthand notes of structures, which claim that not-to-be-understood is meritorious, that not-to-be-there except as a cipher is better than to be there, with the authority of the rational and the easily-read, the easily-seen, the easily-heard.

We in England shall always prefer to leave such things floating about in some public gallery where they are not *bought* (that would be absurd), but eleven thousand pounds is collected and sprinkled over them as 'prizes'—as gifts to good little boys and girls who have the right idea. They stop there just long enough to collect a little dust, to produce a little flutter (and perhaps some outraged foreigner will oblige by attacking an exhibit, the brute); and then they are carted away and will eventually evaporate.

Evaporate—it can be guaranteed that they will do that. For what do you suppose happens to the thousands of *toiles* which are annually assembled in the *Réalités Nouvelles* exhibitions in Paris? They fill the vast halls, hired for the purpose, in the Avenue Président Wilson (which are always empty), and, the exhibition over, they are returned to the artist, who may dwell anywhere in the world from Patagonia to Pakistan.

These distant—do not let us call them painters, but diagrammatists of zero, probably paint over their *œuvre*, and, upon the pure white ground, paint another diagram remarkably like the one they have obliterated. A year hence they will again despatch it to Paris, to '*Réalités Nouvelles*, Avenue Président Wilson, Paris, France'.

How many of us accept Sir Herbert's interpretation of the word 'contemporary'? Not more, perhaps, than one thousand: which is quite a lot, but, among forty million people, an almost invisible minority. In support of what is contemporary for Sir Gerald Kelly, P.R.A., would be a minority, five, or perhaps ten times as numerous as Sir Herbert's. In making use of the word 'contemporary' one must realize, to begin with, how many differing contemporaneous groups there are—some millions strong, and others with no more than a thousand, or even a hundred adherents. It is extremely confusing; but there you are; if you wish to achieve clarity regarding the term 'contemporary', you cannot proceed without allowing for these multiple varieties.

Culturally, of course, there are not forty million people in

England. The great majority are not culturally later than the Paleolithic. The higher functionary of the gas company who has occasionally visited my domicile is probably Neolithic (he reads my books). The taxi-driver I met this morning is certainly Paleo-something—no contemporary of mine, I protest. Could we say there are a hundred thousand of the cultured in England? To arrive at statistics of this sort you would have to decide what you were going to include under the heading 'cultural'. What proportion of the people making use of all the public libraries in Great Britain take out books which have any claim to be 'cultural'? What proportion of the graduates of Oxford and Cambridge have anything to do with culture? The moment you propose to draw up a rough table of cultural groups, with their appropriate numbers, you see how vain it is. All I need do is to remind the reader of the difficulties latent once one proposes to be a little particular in one's use of terms.

To confine oneself to England is a rule one must observe. For, difficult as it is to avoid going astray in England, if you attempt to include the continent of Europe, from Cherbourg to the Bosphorus and so on, in your contemporaneity, you would end in such confusion that you would very soon tear up what you were writing. What is contemporary in culture in places so near together as are France and England is chronologically very different, and never (allowing for the fact that 1914 here is roughly 1884 in Paris) does their contemporaneity coincide. For one hundred years the Anglo-Saxon countries have acquired their musical and their visual authority and directive from France and Germany. The spring fashions ordained by Dior are transmitted to the Anglo-Saxon countries immediately, and they are only valid for half a year. Yet what you see in London and New York is never the same as what you see in Paris: the fashion sent out from Paris is transmuted into something else, and the Parisian contemporaneity never coincides with what is contemporaneous in England or in North America. In the same way, to some extent, the authoritative creations in the fine arts or in music never reach England or America intact. They are received and accepted in atmospheres which considerably modify them, at a date much later than their original creation. The *Pavane pour une Infante Défunte* of Ravel, or the *Pierrot Lunaire* of Schoenberg, when they reach these atmospheres a process of insemination occurs; the English or American flowers, the musical blooms, which are eventually produced conform to local laws which do not coincide with the laws prevailing in their places of origin. They suffer a change as does a gown or a hat. It is the same with the pictures of Modigliani, Bonnard, or Braque, or the sculpture of Brancusi.

3   Sir William Walton by Michael Ayrton

The Leicestershire Education Authority

4   **Man in a Chair by Francis Bacon**

The Hanover Gallery Ltd.

5   Portrait of a Young Woman
     by Robert Colquhoun

Lefevre Gallery

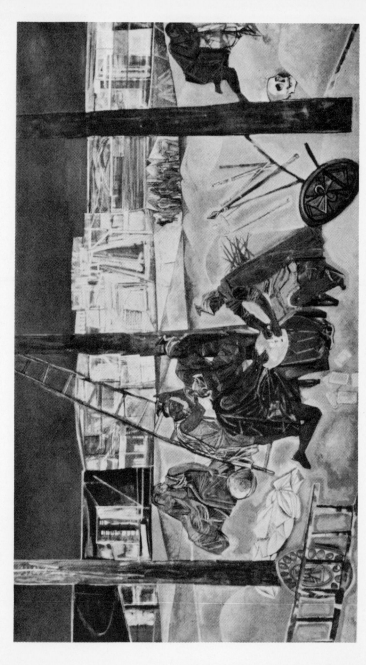

6   The Gamblers by John Minton

Part III

THE PART OF VANITY

XVII

Flattery of the Artist

ONE of the features of contemporary art criticism is un-
doubtedly the amount of flattery the artist comes in for.
He is the hero of a thousand monographs; but less and less
what is of solid advantage to him comes his way. I am now
going to speak of the notion of a *painting animal*: and in that
may be detected a good percentage of self-flattery. This notion
of the painter's ultimately led to a recognition of his right to
exist in a world of his own, and to enjoy a unique autonomy.
In its simplest form the glorious theory of the autonomy of
the painter was adopted in England by Sir Herbert Read.[1]
Such a licence as that imagined for the painter was never
enjoyed by any other craftsman; and the more arcane he can
make his work the more the painter feels himself of a race
apart—a kind of chosen people. And if he gets poorer and
poorer, is not that the destiny of the elect?

Extremism, or such extremism as we meet today, is pathologic. Certain theories or notions are naturally generated in a
period when extremism is almost universally accepted. The
ideal autonomy imagined for the painter, the tendency to
speak as though *what is seen* enjoys a privileged position on
the earth, is characteristic of a time in which theories are substituted for anything real and solid. What, after all, is the
ghastly autonomous privilege, the splendid isolation, about
which I have been speaking, except a private latitude to
do whatever one likes, provided no one else suffers any in-
convenience? Such licences as this, in a time of grandiose

[1] 'But art, I shall maintain, is an autonomous activity . . . as a mode of
knowledge at once its own reality and its own end.' Sir Herbert Read,
p. 2, *Art and Society*.

make-believe like the present, the artist becomes accustomed to, though ultimately he must begin to wonder whether there is no material equivalent for so much hot air. Men who trumpet such theories live in the van of 'culture'; they belong to the camouflaged section of the public services, where with fanfares and resounding words, the absence of culture is gloriously concealed. But this is not the first time I have made it my business to draw attention to the sinister fairy-tale existence lived by the artist, and to show how a palace is built around the starving artist, and a large staff directed to wait upon him, feeding him with praise in place of food.

I began by speaking of the extraordinary amount of flattery the painter absorbs (the pundit, and the rest of the well-paid busy-bodies buzzing around the visual arts responsible, of course, for this). If one were to set about analysing the causes for the present trends in painting and in sculpture, and to catalogue the inducements which are so irresistible that a painter departs from the human society in which he lives and sets himself up in an idealistic desert, vanity and *snobisme* would be the first things to which one would direct one's attention. I am only able to glance at this subject in the present study; but let me take the magnetic word *contemporary*, and analyse a few of its possibilities. Even so habitual and *harmless* an expression as this contains unsuspected potencies when cleverly handled. In the foregoing section this significant word was introduced, and a few of its paradoxical possibilities already indicated. But as I was writing what I did it occurred to me that *Contemporary* was one of those expressions which deserved a good deal of attention.

XVIII

Today the Contemporary = the Extreme

HOW did it come about, you well may ask, that entire
generations of painters have gone to school with abstraction, have acquired a peculiarly barren technique, in which
there are none of the natural delights of interpretation of
nature which have always made painting and drawing and
sculpture so delightful a discipline? A very great part is played
in the conversion to extremism by vanity and *snobisme*. The
desire to be in the swim, to be up to date, to be in step with
fashion in a mild way, is so ordinary a human impulse that a
man need not be called vain, or *snob*, if he gives proof of a
weakness of that kind, especially in a decadence. To like to be
contemporary, to be abreast of the *Zeitgeist*, is surely quite a
harmless weakness, and there is no one who is not, in some
degree, its victim.

Not that contemporaneity is such plain sailing as all that.
Two persons born, on the same day, in the same year, in
Aberdeen and in Canterbury (this is taking an extreme case,
for one might as well say both born within a hundred yards
of one another), are only *contemporaries* in a very limited way.
Some people mature, and some do not; people's interests differ
so widely as to make it impossible to think of them as contemporaries, seeing that the interests of one may have an
extremely Victorian flavour, and the interests of another belong specifically to the present day. Their endowments are very
unequal, and a gifted man does not keep in step with a dull
one. It is quite easy to see how the use of the word *contemporary*
cannot be confined to any one kind of man.

Now the *snobisme* of which I have been speaking causes the
addict to be exquisitely sensitive about the use of that word,

indicating that he belongs to the class from which the *avant-garde* is drawn, namely the word 'contemporary'. Therefore it is an understandable lever, which is why we see that adjective 'contemporary' so often employed in the naming of societies, centres, institutes, etc.

To promise that something will be 'contemporary' is like an assurance of unfailing youth.

And the extremism in the arts—most of all in the visual arts—is a pathological straining after something which boasts of a spectacular *aheadofness*—looking upon the art in question as a *race*. In scientific techniques—in the manufacture of any machine, an automobile, an aeroplane, today more than ever it is a race against the rival manufacturer, because things are so quickly outdated. The press tells us today how our military aeroplanes are lagging behind in the armament race, how we really have no war-plane which is a match for the Russian MiG 15 jet. But one does not have to turn to war industry; wherever machines are being manufactured, there is the atmosphere of a breathless race, where up-to-dateness is a matter of unremitting urgency. And the art-extremist, or, more accurately, the promoters of extremism in art who urge on the painter to more and more extravagance, are behaving as though they mistook the nature of the arts, whose problems are in every way different from those of technology. There must always be competition. That can be seen in the pages of Vasari, and you may recall that, as Van Gogh was approaching his bed with a razor in his hand, Gauguin woke up, and said, 'Vincent, what are you doing? Return to your bed.' Which the Dutchman immediately did. Gauguin possessed great skill, which Van Gogh had not been able to acquire; hence the razor.

All that is natural enough; but a *race*—a race to put as much distance as possible between himself and what everyone else understands or enjoys, *that* is terribly silly.

Now I will return to the word *contemporary*. I do not mean the use of the word involved when someone says to you, is he your contemporary? That of course refers to age. Or here is another instance in which the word *contemporary* is not the *mot juste*. I read the other day Mr. Angus Wilson's interesting book *Hemlock and After*. There are as many homosexuals in its pages as there are normal lovers in a volume of Casanova. Now, it is self-evident that this is *a contemporary book*, because in no novel published in the 'forties, the 'thirties, or the 'twenties would you find homosexuals treated in this way—with amused toleration. It is obvious what kind of a *contemporary* it is.

This identity with a period is not at all what is meant by *cultural* contemporaneity: cultural contemporaneity signifies, according to the painting-extremist, how far you can displace yourself from the cultural centre of things, sticking your little flag up in the iciest and loneliest regions of the intellect.

If you had to frame a definition of the word 'contemporary' you would find, with some surprise, how complex your answer had to be. First, you would ask yourself what was *purely* contemporary. You would have to disentangle it entirely from the past. You would carefully exclude the large volume of something which is *always* going on, and which is much the same in 1854 as in 1954. Then you would have to eliminate anything which just *happens to be occurring* now; for the contemporary should be something which is *essentially* of today.

It must be your problem to isolate what is nineteen-fifty-fourish. But you will be apt to find that, after the most laborious analysis, all you have left is something with the face of yesterday, turning, sometimes quickly and sometimes the reverse, around in a circle.

You will find that your task is often complicated by the intrusion of some material from outside England—for, of course, in defining *the contemporary* you naturally confine yourself to England. If you notice an idea of French origin floating around at a given moment, that cannot be excluded—it is part of the contemporaneity with which you are confronted. It is then necessary to recall that what is contemporary in France in 1910 finally reaches the shores of England by about 1950.

That is always likely to put a strain upon English contemporaneity, and it has to be fitted in with great care. Since the contemporaneity of France and of England do not coincide, at a time when there happens to be more Gallic influence than usual it would be found almost impossible to arrive at a definition of what is 'contemporary'.

I will leave your supposed attempt to define what is contemporary, however, and simply enquire what in your view is the most contemporary kind of painting in England at the present moment. It would be quite impossible to answer that unless one had agreed on a definition of the contemporary. If one had agreed that the answer to the question would be found by identifying the artist who, in his practice, was most distant from, let us say, Picasso—most distant in a direction never trod by human foot before—then that could be automatically ascertained, and there would never be any problem at all. But if a less mechanical fashion was in vogue, and to be contemporary could not be decided in that simple way, one's task might in that case be very difficult.

There is one thing which has not so far been mentioned, and that is, *how many people* have any claim to the status of *contemporary*? For instance, 'are the fifty million English alive in 1954 more *contemporary* because of Sir Herbert?' This is another way of putting the question. Another question of the same sort: 'Is France more contemporary because of the existence in its capital city of *la Réalités Nouvelles*?' The answer to any such question is that France possesses no contemporaneity, and that England does not either. Contemporaneity is so small a thing, applying to so limited a number of people, that it cannot be spoken of in connection with a nation.

On the other hand, there are, perhaps, five or six thousand contemporary people in Great Britain; which means that there are that number who aspire to be contemporary. The 'contemporary' is a cultural élite. The élite of 1950 in England is the same as the élite of 1910 in France, and of Germany in 1920. And a very restricted amount of éliteness is always existing everywhere. So the 'contemporary' has nothing to do with time, nor with age. The 'contemporary' of Sir Herbert's institute has been in existence, in one place and another, for the entire century; which is why it has nothing to do with time, although it is generally supposed to mean *today*.

Extremism = contemporary. I do not see how you could get nearer to the meaning of contemporary than that. Although one thinks of extremism as something perpetually moving forward (violently progressing), that is an illusion. Extremism may be doing that, but far more often it is stationary. Or there may be some inconsequential movement, just enough to create the illusion that something is happening, although in reality nothing is happening. In both sculpture and painting, when extremism has been standing still for two or three decades, it gets to look more and more academic, less and less extreme. It will only be when that childish sport is abandoned that something really *new* will appear in the visual arts.

XIX

The Glamour of the Extreme

EXTREMISM in all its forms, and in every department of life, has a glamorous attraction for a certain type of man, as it has everywhere that attraction for youth. In politics is where this glamour proves most dangerous.

I have a friend who is a natural bourgeois. He was the son of a minor Eminence. At the university, during the fellow-travelling decade, he got in the habit of talking big and bloody about social revolution. He was not intelligent or mentally mature enough to understand the guillotine and the firing-squad; he had not even read Karl Marx. But for the rest of his life, and he is now over fifty, he has remained a sort of undergraduate communist, simply because it secured for him a claim to superiority which he coveted, and could obtain in no other way, anything like as easily as that.

My friend is a little monster of vanity. He is always showing off; if there were a fire he would jump about among the little flames where he thought it was safe, and would order every-body about as if he were a Fire Captain. At least no one could fail to understand what made him a pseudo-communist.

Extremities of thought or of feeling may almost scorch the paper upon which something is printed, but in literary expression the *form* remains intact, the words *cad* or *unspeakable blackguard* get printed with as much decorum as *please pass the salt*. In literature, I am very happy to say, there is no danger so far of a crusade to stampede the entire writing world into an uproarious dumbness, or the next thing to it. Miss Stein did her best with an infectious stammer. One would have thought she would have misled a few dozen weak-minded young men in her native land; but as far as I know there were no followers.

If, however, you see some literary man 'go abstract' and begin writing dumb, pay no attention, any more than you would to a child going 'Puff Puff!', imagining himself a locomotive. Vanity is responsible for a good deal of youthful homicide. Some late-teenaged boys were arrested not long ago 'in connection' with the death of a twenty-one-year-old. It might be an extra-young racing gang, or it might be the outcome of a desire-to-shine in the gutters of some suburb. An extremist, perhaps, who needs a corpse to bolster his reputation for toughness, and to show himself a fellow who is prepared to go *as far as anyone can.*

But I am not putting down to a *desire-to-shine* all extremism in painting or sculpture. Sometimes an absence of talent may wish to conceal itself; any fantastic mess will serve the purpose; or it can masquerade in a rhomboid and a bunch of triangles. And then there is (an even rarer bird) a man of the golden mean. But in that there is no advertisement. However, I have sufficiently illustrated this little point, and shall wind up by observing that excess or extreme and vanity are closely related.

Part IV

ERRORS OF MALRAUX

XX

'A Compact Exclusive Clan'

IN the visual arts the extremism of the first half of the
twentieth century is, ostensibly, a continuation of the experi-
mental character of painting during the second half of the
nineteenth century. In fact, however, the new twentieth-
century advances are quite different in character from that
of the period of which they are supposed to be a logical con-
tinuance. For instance, the Cubism of Picasso is spoken of as
a development of the work of Cézanne. If it were only *that*, we
should still be at the heart of painting, instead of outside and
beyond it.

In the future, the historian will immediately be struck by
the abrupt change that came over painting in the second of
these groups of fifty years, successive and continuous as they
were in time and space. To that historian the first of this pair
of half-centuries, beginning with Manet and Monet, and ending
with Gauguin and Vuillard, will seem to be in a sunlit stretch
of time, given over gloriously to the art of painting; whereas
the half-century which has just come to a close will appear a
dark and feverish march of new schools, at its heart metaphysical, and far from the sunlit earth of 'Le bon bock', or of
Monet's 'Boulevard des Capucines, Paris.' This stark difference
might be explained by the fact that in the twentieth century
the guiding spirits in painting were not Frenchmen. Picasso,
at one time, was almost *everything* in France; when someone
asked him what the young men were doing, he answered, 'La
jeunesse c'est moi,' which was a quite accurate description of
the situation. I merely mention this; the change from the
national to the international could hardly afford a full explanation for the metamorphosis.

It is an interesting speculation to ask oneself to what the above historian would attribute the nineteenth-century ferment in the visual arts. It does not seem to me that there is anything obscure about the causes of what happened in French art in the last century. But there are theories about this, held by 'art historians' of the present day, which seem to me to apply, possibly, to our own half-century, and not to that which began roughly with the French Impressionists. This mistake, as it seems to me, may be the result of regarding our century, visually, as a mere continuation of the last.

An admirably illustrated, two volume, art-historical study by the novelist, André Malraux, has recently appeared. The date of publication in France was 1949; it will be from the translation of this work, published by Pantheon Books, New York [1] that I shall be quoting. Malraux has a lot to say on the subject of the insulation of the visual artist, and at this point I should like, accompanied by rather extensive quotation, to examine what he says.

At several places in the course of these two volumes, Malraux refers to artists as a 'sect' or as a 'caste'. Thus, on page 134, Vol. I, where he is speaking of the period of the first great artistic innovations in France, he writes, 'For now the artists were becoming a caste.' And a little lower down on the same page, 'From the end of the eighteenth century, though the various arts diverged, the artists themselves formed a compact, exclusive clan and launched concerted attacks on the culture of which they disapproved. Art had changed its character; from being a mere adornment of civilization, it was becoming what we now mean by art.'

Here you have the specifically *political* explanation of this phenomenon—the large and aggressive sect of craftsmen of the visual arts, 'a compact, exclusive clan', on the march against

[1] The English edition of M. Malraux's work, *The Voices of Silence*, is published in London by Secker & Warburg, Ltd. and represents the author's recension of *Le Psychologie d'Art*.

all the cultural standards of their time—against bourgeois
standards, according to Malraux, as if their attack were
political. More and more, their pictures were looked upon as
bombs, to hurl at the possessing class. In my view the nineteenth-century painters were not a political sect, but a com-
munity of painters; the explosive nature of their pictures was
not destined to blast society, but to destroy the pictures of the
school which preceded theirs. Like other men, they thought
about politics, about what was going on around them: and,
since there was nothing to cause them to arrange their thinking, they no doubt had a very low opinion of the politicians
of the republics and empires succeeding to the Napoleonic epic.
On the other hand, whatever their view of the régime, that
played no part in their experimenting with *pointillisme*, or of
the Impressionist theories of which that was a development.

The men of letters were, to a large extent, on the march also,
but they did not form anything that could be described as a
compact and considerable body of dissidents like the artists,
and they were never technical extremists in the way the
painters were. The same might be said of musicians—who, for
the kind of reason indicated in Section III, were less disposed
to defy the society to which they belonged.

The passage quoted above ends with the words 'what we
now mean by art'. What exactly 'we' refers to here is un-
certain; but Malraux is inclined to endow the visual arts with
mystical revolutionary attributes. He casts 'art' for the rôle of
destroyer of bourgeois values. It is necessary to recall that
Malraux has himself played the part of an extreme kind of
fellow-traveller; which, of course, in a general way, does not
invalidate his criticism, these two volumes of his containing
much excellent popularizing, of special use where he is writing
of the art of classical Greece and its influence in the Orient.
Then, after all, ever since the French Revolution, in things
even as remote from politics as pictures of apples or sun-
flowers, there *are* no doubt vibrations originating in the Terror.

XXI

The Coming of non-Humanistic Art

WHATEVER our view of these things may be, in the
fine arts the nineteenth century began with the rise
of a militant romanticism, unquestionably (1) reflecting the
violences of the Revolution, and (2) imbued with iconoclastic
fire and defiance of all authority. Opposed to this were such
classicists as Ingres (pupil of David), standing for the old order
and for the cultural inheritance of Europe. So, from the start,
there was a civil war from one end to the other of the studios.
Then, mid-way in the nineteenth century, began, with the
Impressionists, that definitely quite new attitude of painters
towards the pictures they painted. They no longer painted
them in order to please patron or public, but to please themselves, and imbued with a belief in the missionary destiny of
painting (the gospel of *l'art pour l'art*, which is a gospel hostile
to politics). I agree that to give proof of religious zeal where
nothing but art was at stake is very odd, for they depended
upon these pictures for their bread and butter, but there it is.
With the greatest enthusiasm some of them began an attempt
to paint the sunlight; the public laughed angrily at the result,
looking upon their pictures as incomprehensible daubs. And so
the revolt began; and from the time of Monet, Pissarro, and
their friends, almost without a break, down to the present day,
to Picasso and his followers, painters have apparently done
their best to displease and startle the public instead of painting
pictures which had a reasonable chance of selling.

Artists persuaded a limited number of people to buy their
canvases, critics and picture dealers insisting upon the likelihood of these revolutionary canvases selling for vast sums of
money in the immediate future, and, apart from that, being

great works of art, which a man should be proud to hang upon
his walls. So, for about a century, painters, in spite of their
unaccommodating attitude, have succeeded in making a pre-
carious living (a small number a very good living, even).[1] But
the world-wars and revolutions which began in the second
decade of this century have, at last, so shattered the economies
of Europe and modified the outlook of those societies which
remain, that the artist, painter or sculptor finds it increasingly
difficult to make anything like a regular living (from painting
increasingly disagreeable pictures or producing more and more
eccentric pieces of sculpture), and André Malraux, as a sup-
porter of universal revolution—and not himself a painter or a
sculptor—regards this situation with unquestioning approval.

Humanism is for Malraux an arch-enemy; as a critic he
stands squarely in the centre of the anti-human bloc. He
describes how formerly artists were satisfied to co-operate with
humanism, but now they will co-operate with absolutely nothing, for there is nothing there which a true artist would
touch with a barge-pole. But let me quote.

Humanistic art had made much of the culture to which it belonged, but with the coming of non-humanistic art, which stood on
its own rights, artists were drawn together all the more intimately
as a result of art's estrangement from the culture, and the society,
of their time. In this oasis of art—without a precedent, even in
Florence—art became an activity for which life furnished no more
than the raw material, and a man made good his status by his
power of bodying forth a world created by himself. So there came
into being not so much a religion as a fanatically devoted sect . . .
regarding its saints (and its eccentrics, too) as the Salt of the Earth;
more gratified, like all sects, than its votaries admitted by the
clandestine nature of their activities, and prepared to suffer, if
needs were, in the Cause of a Truth none the less cogent for its
vagueness. (Vol. I, p. 135.)

As you will see from this, there is, in the view of this

---

[1] Where I use the word *artist* or *painter* I refer to serious artists; I use the
expression *pot-boiler* for the commercial variety.

observer, something very peculiar about the visual artist. Imagine if writers, or if musicians, formed themselves into a 'clandestine' sect, dedicating themselves to some 'truth', prepared to suffer the hardship which this must entail. Imagine if they always wrote books which were either displeasing or incomprehensible to their fellow-citizens. For, according to Malraux, these technical extremisms of the painters and sculptors, the visual artist, are not, as is generally supposed, a question of *ways of painting pictures*, but of ways of thinking, of political belief. They desire to overturn the ethos of the nation to which they belong.

I was a painter, a visual artist, and at the beginning of my career I began by painting pictures of an extremist nature, and indulging in propaganda for visual extremism. What I *thought* I was doing was developing new methods of pictorial expression; but I should have been told by the critics who think like Malraux that all this was much more to do with something quite untechnical, and not concerned specifically with the visual arts.

These critics would, of course, be writers, journalists probably, and all they knew or cared about the painter's art would be nil; it would naturally be impossible for them to imagine anyone valuing more highly a few dabs of paint, or a few scratches of a pen, than the battles for the mastery of the world. It is quite understandable that they should think you were fooling if you disowned any political aim. When I read Malraux I know that his observation in matters concerning the visual arts must necessarily be defective. It would be natural to him to suppose that a painter was (like himself) fired by politics, when this painter was, in reality, 'mad about drawing', as was Hokusai, or mad about certain combinations of black and white, as was one of Malraux's favourites, Franz Hals. His is a defect like a defective ear, which might lead a man to think that Hindemith was harbouring some secret design (not musical at all), instead of existing in a dimension similar to that of the mathematician, and equally incorruptible. From

long experience I am able to say that, while artists are naturally
prone to experiment, and to try new methods of expression,
there is, identifying himself with the artist, the promoter and
inspirer of 'movements', who is often motivated by political
enthusiasm. The artist is apt to be credited with the politics of
the promoter. Lastly, for the picture to be complete, instances
can be found of painters who are politically very active.
Camille Pissarro, one of the most perfervid inspirers of Impressionism, and then of the movement which followed it, was,
certainly, a politician; but Degas, Manet, Toulouse-Lautrec,
Gauguin, on the other hand, to name only a few, were actuated
in what they did by art first and foremost, and with the great
majority of painters this was the case. Manet, to whom Malraux
is constantly referring, and who is regarded by him as the *first*
of the new kind of artists, was a great traditionalist, setting up
Velasquez as a model, in opposition to the vulgarity and bad
painting of the Salons. Gauguin was a pure romantic, going
Indian, and claiming to be, through his mother, half Indian
himself. And I cannot help thinking that Malraux, as a critic,
has been too much influenced by his friends among the painters
of what we call the *École de Paris*.

Another very important point is that Malraux entirely
ignores various factors, counting for a great deal in the life of
the visual artist during the past hundred years. In the last
century, for instance, the coming of the photograph was an
event of far greater importance for the visual artist than has
been the cinematograph, in the present century, for the actor.
Malraux writes (with reference to the new attitude of the
painter dramatically illustrated by the Impressionist Movement), 'Now all that was changed; firstly, because the spectator, who asked for 'finished' pictures, would have none of a
way of seeing which was just seeing and no more; and especially
because the Impressionists, far from desiring the spectator's
assent, disclaimed it. Like the Byzantines, they disowned
the public. . . .' And this is quite true; but Malraux gives the
wrong reasons for these phenomena. As a fellow-traveller, the

eighteenth century was for him the French Revolution, only that. For the historian of the future the Industrial Revolution will overshadow the great political explosion in France. The artists of the second half of the nineteenth century had moved deep into the industrial age, of which the invention of the camera was an integral part. Along with the aftermath of the French Revolution (which affected things for the bad as well as for the good), the Industrial Revolution rapidly resulted in a vulgarization of the whole of society from which we still suffer—the Hollywood cinema is something which could not have existed prior to the industrial age. The culture against which, according to Malraux, the visual artists were violently reacting was, certainly, in a sense, the vulgarity of the bourgeoisie (the communist bogey, for which the French language is *de rigueur*), and the vulgarity of those artists who pandered to it, *and* to the vulgarity of everyone else and everything else. But what was the cause of this vulgarity? *It was the natural result of the industrial age*; and that fact is completely ignored not only by Malraux, but by every other art historian of the same political bias as his, who much prefer to point to the French Revolution.

Let me conclude my criticism of this part of Malraux's study by commenting upon what he describes as the 'Elect Order of World-forsakers'. We all at some time have read O'Shaughnessy's poem about the 'world-losers and world-forsakers'. In it this romantic Irishman asserts that the poet, solitary and unworldly, is in fact 'the mover and shaker of the world forever it seems'. In the course of the poem you may read the words,

> We...
> Built Nineveh with our sighing,
> And Babel itself with our mirth.

Now it is well enough to see in the man of words, words that possess so magical a power, the man ideally solitary, world-losing and world-forsaking, but possessed of a power to shake the earth from one pole to the other. Jean-Jacques Rousseau, with his books, certainly did that—tore up society by the roots. But an oil-painting, or, however beautiful, an ink-drawing, cannot do things of that kind. Paul Cézanne can revolutionize the manner of painting of a generation or two of painters; but it is quite impossible for his canvases to have any effect outside of the technique of painting. The man who wrote the words of the song used in the French Revolution, *Saint Nicholas a trois clériaux*, can set men chanting with diabolic glee around the guillotines; but a plate of Cézanne's apples could not even stimulate a man's hunger.

XXII

Superficiality of Cultures

AMONG the various types of creator, the visual artist is certainly one of the most inaccessible to the man in the street. I mean by this, that, in looking at what he has done, the painter sees one thing, the public another; and to train up the public so that they see the *same* thing is impossible. This is because what the painter sees is in another dimension altogether.

I will now turn again to André Malraux, to that part of his work where he declares that the population at large has not, in the modern age of Europe, participated in cultural change. He repudiates the notion of a Gothic, a Renaissance, or a Baroque *period*—when everyone, butcher and baker and candlestick-maker, was Gothic-minded, or Baroque-minded, and so on. He asserts that the vast majority of the European population has, during the past millennium, continued just the same, quite unaltered by the fact that scholar and priest were enthusiastically occupied, for instance, with the literature, philosophy, the visual arts of Greek antiquity, and the fact that painters, sculptors, and architects were busy building up the style, later to be known as the Italian Renaissance.

Now, it was quite unnecessary for Malraux to repudiate the theory in question, for it is self-evident that no culture in the modern age has penetrated very deep. We are not a Pacific Island population. We exist in layers, and have done so since a semi-primitive time; if a culture suffused the inferior layers, it would certainly not be dominating the upper layers. But let me appeal to history.

The historian assures us, to take what Malraux would, I think, accept as a parallel case, that the Wars of the Roses, in

England, was a matter in which the nobles were interested, but nobody else. Indeed, international trade prospered to an unusual extent.

In European history such paradoxes are rather the rule than the exception. For instance, Napoleon's invasion of Russia provides an excellent example. Without referring to history one would be inclined to think that the Russian people must have been shaken from top to bottom by that sensational event, including the occupation of their principal city. In fact,[1] this, apparently, was not the case. Only the court and the army and the countryside through which the Napoleonic columns advanced and retreated—and Moscow, of course—paid any attention to it. The balls and festivities of the aristocratic life proceeded as usual, in all parts of Russia out of reach of the French army.

If a military invasion of a country, or if a civil war, are events in which the majority of the population do not participate, then certainly it is easy to understand how a cultural 're-birth', or renaissance, and the development of a new style in painting, did not influence the butcher, the baker, and the candlestick-maker. Where a style in the visual arts, like the Gothic, is identified with religion, it is to some extent a different matter, at a moment of universal belief, in an 'age of faith'. Nevertheless, the particular *style* involved, in the matter of architecture, or the other visual arts, would not very greatly concern the bulk of the population.

We may agree that the general run of men are a fairly constant factor, going on with their lives unaffected by such things as Romanesque, Baroque—or Impressionist, or Surrealist styles in art. There is no difficulty about conceding that the craftsman, in one of the more intellectual forms of art, will, in the nature of things, pay very little attention to the majority of the population. That he should be a 'law unto himself' is only another step, but this final step, realizing an absolute autonomy for a craftsman, is quite different from all the other steps.

[1] Cf. *War and Peace*, Leo Tolstoy.

As I have now restored this question of the autonomy of
the craftsman in a fine art to its realistic status, let me, before
concluding, list the ultimate issues. (1) There is the question
of whether the visual artist is alone in the world. (2) As to
whether a craft, like any other human activity, completely
inaccessible to other men, is of any value, superior to that of
a private amusement? (3) Whether this boast of absolute
autonomy could be advanced (by pundits) for an art or craft
at any period except one in which the art or craft is defunctive,
and has nothing further to expect of the rest of the population,
and is now an academic showpiece, in a propagandist sideshow
marked CULTURE?

Let us examine question (1). The craftsman of one of the
visual arts is not economically independent. This is a separate
question, since it is intellectual or craftsmanly autonomy
which is involved. Yet to be an artist at all—seriously, which
means all the time—a man's economic requirements must be
assured.

Next, the visual artist cannot be regarded as alone, in any
sense, for he lives in society, and if the work he did were looked
upon as dangerous or in any way as objectionable, or anti-
social, he would be forcibly discouraged.

If your view is that the artist's life is similar to that of a
bird (as it were a *painting sparrow*) as is the case with some
people, then his mental faculties are not in question. But the
painter and the sculptor *think*, in a way unknown to a sparrow;
they read books—optical treatises, like the Impressionists;
books of physics, like the Cubists; books of Surrealist theory,
or of Freudian psychology, like the Surrealists. And all artists
of this century have been catered for by an unflagging stream
of books about themselves, or to satisfy their special interests.
The modern artist may be said to find the literary atmosphere
as necessary as is oxygen for the mountaineer engaged in
high-altitude climbing.

Then, is he indifferent to the public? As women are said to
dress purely for other women, does the artist never think of

anything but other artists? This is, of course, not the case. If it is true, as we have seen, that artists live in one world, and the butcher, the baker, the candlestick-maker in another, that is not the end of the story: for they are not the only kind of people in the world. The artist, or the craftsman—sculptor or painter—is not alone in the world with the butcher, the baker, the candlestick-maker, as if they had been shipwrecked upon an island.

No. There is not only a Gothic, a Renaissance,—a 'classic' or a romantic—painter, sculptor, or architect. In these cultures, when a cultivated public exists, the artist may be quite independent of the butcher, the baker, the candlestick-maker, but not otherwise. The cultivated public is often very large, for the businessman, the politician, the man of science, the product of the universities, the courtier (where there is a court), monasteries (when there were monasteries), etc., swell it, each in one degree or another. In our own time, the visual artist and the writer, these two classes of citizen alone, provide a (more or less) cultivated public formidable in size. And without the members of this cultivated class no art could exist. If the only people in the world were the butcher, the baker, the candlestick-maker—the small businessman (creative or uncreative), the mass of the labouring class and so on, there would be no fine art or any other art. Malraux rather tends to forget this supremely important fact.

XXIII

The Diabolical Principle

IT must have seemed that I could find nothing in Malraux to agree with. But there are indications throughout the two massive books from which I have been quoting that Malraux does not always think quite the same; indeed, he does at times seem (at least at first) to be thinking very much as I do. Let me quote a passage of brilliant insight, where he seems to be saying the last word about the collective movements which have dominated this century. It is from Volume II, page 124, and it refers, among other things, to the diabolical principle (a title I have used for one of my earlier books).

Artists attacking all humanistic values (i.e., all engaged in total attack upon humanistic values) challenge implicitly the civilization which gave them birth or brings them back to life. That, indeed, is the link between the naive and the early mediaeval artist; between the madman (sometimes the child as well) and the primitive. And that is what makes each of these arts a weapon in the armoury of modern anti-humanism. The artist who goes to school with the primitives obviously seeks more than a mere discovery of forms. In a culture like ours every recourse to primitivism implies a fellowship with what our culture lacks. And our revival of these forms, like our appreciation of them, carries with it an appeal to forces latent below the conscious threshold.... Raphael's world—the world of man at peace with God—had, since the death of Ingres, become an alien, hostile world, and the School of Bologna ... strikes us ... as an imposture.... But already the gods of the day—which their art ignored—had mustered their attendant devils; history, whose importunity now obsesses Europe, much as Buddha's pyrrhonism disintegrated Asia, was coming into being. No longer was it mere chronology but an anxious investigation of a past for any light it might throw on the dark vistas of the future. Western culture was losing faith in itself. The diabolical principle—from war, that major devil, to its train of minor devils, fears and complexes— which is present more or less surreptitiously in all savage art, was coming to the fore again. . . . That diabolical principle stands for all in man that seeks to compass his destruction. The powers of darkness of the Christian past, the Freudian devil, and the devil of Bikini—all wear the same aspect. And the more ground these new demons gain in Europe, the more her art tends to hark back to the mood of earlier cultures plagued by their appropriate devils. . . . By contrast with the nineteenth, our century stands for a Renaissance of Destiny. This Europe of phantom cities is not more devastated than is the idea of Man that once was hers.

Malraux analyses very well the art-scene of our time. He groups primitivism (African, Sumerian, etc.), infantilism, the art of the lunatic, as well as that of the Child. He sees the diabolic principle inhering in the grouping. I could not, myself, have dissected with more understanding the major impetus responsible for much of the painting, sculpture, and design in our time. God is dead, Sartre asserts; and so does Malraux. But the latter perceives the Devil brought in by some of the contemporary artists and he applauds the coming back into currency of the diabolic. This is not surprising, seeing that, in much of his literary work, he rather preens himself, one feels, upon his diabolism. Where Malraux and I differ is that I am not one of those who climb upon the band wagon of the Fiend. But I applaud Malraux's advertisement of the true position. As I read this I was delighted to find how almost identical was his analysis of this period of concentrated decadence with my own. But I laughed, of course; for, both of us seeing the same thing, I had found it bad (seeing that I am the reverse of a diabolist); whereas Malraux registered how all these tendencies and sub-movements cohered, as I would group the virtues of a man for whom I had a good deal of esteem.

POSTSCRIPT

Conclusion

EXTREMISM—or the affectation of extremism—is no longer disapproved of by any member of that public who before the last war could be depended on noisily to disparage anything violent and displeasing in any of the arts. After all, the people who buy pictures to hang on their walls grow fewer and fewer. Taxation has put that little habit out of reach of the great majority; yet undiminished crowds visit the exhibitions of the Royal Academy, and the shows to be seen at the various dealers. There is still a surprisingly large class of people who are known among their friends as knowledgeable about pictures, and liable even to buy some juicy little millstream, or summer-scene on the Norfolk Broads. The buying has almost stopped (though the prices of contemporary pictures have become disgustingly reasonable), but the 'interest' persists. Now I do not say that this large class of 'art-loving' bourgeoisie approves of the extremist fashions, but quite recently it has been noticeable how a new toleration has crept into their attitude. The fact is that this impoverished herd does not wish to be held responsible for keeping art going. If all that is dynamic in art, and so seeming to claim support, hanged itself by the heels, or hid in some distant cave, or sailed away like Hiawatha into some unknown region, then all would be well. The 'art-lover's' conscience would be at rest. It is much the same thing if the modernists pushed themselves so far out of reach of the human norm that no one could be expected to accompany them.

If the *Réalités Nouvelles* exhibitions in Paris were generally accepted as 'Art Today', well, that would be a solution. No one could reasonably be described as barbarous, and wanting in all artistic sensibility, if he did not immediately rush to the Avenue Président Wilson and purchase two or three of these pictures. They are rigidly abstract, and that is admittedly only for the extreme initiate. Why this would be a happy solution is, among other things, because no one has the money or even the will, to buy pictures, and yet no one is prepared just to say 'the arts belong to the past, and especially easel-pictures—oil-paintings'.

You see, all this is fitting in very nicely. The more intelligent dealers understand very well that in the welfare state—the *full* welfare state—there will not be much for them to do. If capitalism disappears, the picture dealers disappear too, and so it is not so surprising as it may at first seem that many of these gentlemen take a plunge into zero, as it were; hold exhibitions of pictures which are so abstract, and often tamely and dully so. It is in Paris that this chiefly occurs; otherwise dealers of course just go on selling the 'gilt-edged' or some pretty little line which they hope may still attract the gilded passer-by, American or other, from what has been called the 'bankers' republic'.

So much for the public. What of the governments? Oh, *they* ask nothing better than that the vital principle in the visual arts should fly away to some equally repulsive and inaccessible regions, where it would no longer be anybody's responsibility. They are even prepared to regard as a benefactor any Pied Piper, or Mad Hatter, or anyone else who leads the troublesome sect of artists away into the wilderness, and there persuades them to remain, scratching a little image, or rather some symbolical figure in the sands.

So who on earth is such a book as this written for? The general public, I trust, will not begin by reading this conclusion. It will, I hope, be interested to see the true meaning of extremism in the visual arts put on record by an artist: for, however much it may tolerate the extremist absurdities resorted to by the painter or the sculptor, nevertheless a good fund of malice is always stored up against the artist, as much demented as in his right mind. I must rely on this, and for the rest my book is written for that small number of artists whose interests lie in the van of the true advance, but who would sooner see the great civilized art abdicate in the presence of chaos, rather than commit a clownish suicide.

Part V

CONCLUSION

Postscript

WE are told that it is now so costly to print a book in New York, that no publisher dare risk the production of an unorthodox or non-best-selling type (which are apt to be the most worth while to publish). That results in the book trade having now fallen to the same abysmal level as the cinema, where, as we know, the celluloid is so fabulously expensive that only the films of the vulgarest type can be undertaken in Hollywood.

In England things have not reached the same level as in the United States in those industries upon which some great cultural activity depends. But there is an exception to this, namely the theatre. The rental of a theatre in London at the present moment entails so enormous an expense that the quality of stage performances is restricted to plays of the most insignificant and popular kind, with rare exceptions. For anyone interested in this subject I recommend a recently published book, *The Unholy Trade*, by Richard Findlater.

Bearing all this and much more of the same kind in mind, it is not difficult to foretell what the cultural standards of our sons, and still more grandsons, will be like.

If the cost of living must forever rise, it is equally a law of this time that the cultural standard must continue to fall. As you see a pound of coffee rising in price, you may be sure that, at the same time, the quality of painting or music is taking a drop downhill of the same amount. Therefore, anything one may say about the declining vitality in one art can be applied to every other art. The arts I have chosen for analysis in the race towards disintegration may be far ahead of some other art; but that will only be momentary.

If things were to go on evenly and uneventfully it would be easy to predict what point the world would have reached in one hundred, or two hundred years from now. But no man can predict anything at this stage of the world's history, no politician, no financier, no technician. We live in the period of the great suspense. Why I can say no more than what is to be read in the above treatise is because of the laws obtaining in the great suspense.

We seem to be running down, everywhere in life, to a final end to all good things. Compared to fifty years ago, when the supreme and ultimate rot began, our food—our milk, our cheese, our bread, our concocted foods, everything, in short, is inferior, and there is every reason to suppose that it will get more so, decade by decade. The cloth our clothes are made of has declined in quality, not only in beauty but in durability, to such an extent that no tailor would have the face to deny it. The furniture at present manufactured, the materials with which our houses are built, the bricks, the mortar, the wood, the fittings, are notoriously inferior to what they were a short century ago. Paper is not what it was, in our newspapers, our books, our writing materials and so on; steel products, such as scissors, pins, etc., become less and less reliable; the gut used in surgical stitching is no longer graded; but it is not necessary to enumerate this decline in detail. Everything that is sold in the shops is necessarily inferior to what it was so short a time ago as twelve months. Why? For the very good reason that the word *business* may be defined as buying cheap and selling dear. Mr. Franklin Delano Roosevelt insisted that 'The business man is a crook.' He is, by definition, dishonest. The board meetings and conferences in every business establishment concern themselves always with some essentially dishonest device for putting more money in their pockets; in the case of the manufacturers, the subject discussed is how, in manufacturing their speciality, they may cheat the public—to make the public pay the same price (or more) for an article composed of less valuable ingredients. This must involve a progressive deterioration of everything we buy, from the gas in our meters to the socks on our feet.

Meanwhile, the great suspense is a factor of daily, unrelenting ruin. The enormous cost entailed by the fabulous armaments imposed on both sides in the preparation for the *next* war is alone sufficient to bleed us white, to maintain a dangerous fever in all our blood; and, since the arms we are now manufacturing are potentially so destructive that when at length they are used they may entirely alter our lives, they are responsible for the great suspense.

Well. Unless human beings are going to experience the same deterioration in the very tissues of which their bodies are composed, unless their skins are to lose their resilience, their warmth, and all the other qualities which make them so high class a covering for a man to have; unless nature is to begin to take less trouble over our nails, our hair (that may disappear altogether), our wonderful shining eyes, which may become dull and myopic, so that spectacles must be provided for all from the cradle onwards—unless all this is to come about there will have to be some great revolution. That is why talking about the alarming outlook for the fine arts appears so trivial a matter when one has finished writing about it. It is infected with the triviality of everything else.